BIOLOGY

PIONEERS in SCIENCE

BIOLOGY

The People Behind the Science

KATHERINE CULLEN, PH.D.

CHELSEA HOUSE
PUBLISHERS
An imprint of Infobase Publishing

Biology: The People Behind the Science

Chelsea House
An imprint of Infobase Publishing
132 West 31st Street
New York NY 10001

For Library of Congress Cataloging-in-Publication Data, please contact the publisher.

ISBN 0-8160-5461-4

Chelsea House books are available at special discounts when purchased in bulk quantities for businesses, associations, institutions, or sales promotions. Please call our Special Sales Department in New York at (212) 967-8800 or (800) 322-8755.

You can find Chelsea House on the World Wide Web at
http://www.chelseahouse.com

Text design by Mary Susan Ryan-Flynn
Cover design by Cathy Rincon
Illustrations by Bobbi McCutcheon

Printed in the United States of America

MP FOF 10 9 8 7 6 5 4 3 2 1

This book is printed on acid-free paper.

*I dedicate this book to
all future pioneers in science.*

☙

CONTENTS

PREFACE

Being first in line earns a devoted fan the best seat in the stadium. The first runner to break the ribbon spanning the finish line receives a gold medal. The firstborn child inherits the royal throne. Certain advantages or privileges often accompany being the first, but sometimes the price paid is considerable. Neil Armstrong, the first man to walk on the Moon, began flying lessons at age 16, toiled at numerous jobs to pay tuition, studied diligently to earn his bachelor's degree in aerospace engineering, flew 78 combat missions in Korea as a brave navy pilot, worked as a civilian test pilot for seven years, then as an astronaut for NASA for another seven years, and made several dangerous trips into space before the historic *Apollo 11* mission. He endured rigorous physical and mental preparation, underwent years of training, and risked his life to courageously step foot where no man had ever walked before. Armstrong was a pioneer of space exploration; he opened up the way for others to follow. Not all pioneering activities may be as perilous as space exploration. But like the ardent fan, a pioneer in science must be dedicated; like the competitive runner, she must be committed; and like being born to royalty, sometimes providence plays a role.

Science encompasses all knowledge based on general truths or observed facts. More narrowly defined, science refers to a branch of knowledge that specifically deals with the natural world and its laws. Philosophically described, science is an endeavor, a search for truth, a way of knowing, or a means of discovering. Scientists gain information through employing a procedure called the scientific method. The scientific method requires one to state the problem and formulate a testable hypothesis or educated guess to describe a phenomenon or explain an observation, test the hypothesis experimentally or by collecting data from observations, and draw conclusions from the results. Data can eliminate a hypothesis, but never confirm it with absolute certainty; scientists may accept a hypothesis as true when sufficient supporting evidence has been obtained. The process sounds entirely straightforward, but sometimes advancements in science do not follow such a logical approach. Because humans make the observations, generate the hypothesis, carry out the experiments, and draw the conclusions, students of science must recognize the personal dimension of science.

Pioneers in Science is a set of volumes that profile the people behind the science, individuals who initiated new lines of thought or research. They risked possible failure and often faced opposition but persisted to pave new pathways of scientific exploration. Their backgrounds vary tremendously; some never graduated from secondary school, while others earned multiple advanced degrees. Familial affluence allowed some to pursue research unhindered by financial concerns, but others were so poor they suffered from malnutrition or became homeless. Personalities ranged from exuberant to somber and gentle to stubborn, but they all sacrificed, giving their time, insight, and commitment because they believed in the pursuit of knowledge. The desire to understand kept them going when they faced difficulties, and their contributions moved science forward.

The set consists of eight separate volumes: *Biology; Chemistry; Earth Science; Marine Science; Physics; Science, Technology, and Society; Space and Astronomy;* and *Weather and Climate.* Each book contains 10 biographical sketches of pioneering individuals in a subject, including information about their childhood, how they entered into their scientific careers, their research, and enough background science information for the reader to appreciate their discoveries and contributions. Though all the profiled individuals are certainly distinguished, their inclusion is not intended to imply that they are the greatest scientists of all time. Rather, the profiled individuals were selected to reflect a variety of subdisciplines in each field, different histories, alternative approaches to science, and diverse characters.

Each chapter includes a chronology and a list of specific references about the individual and his work. Each book also includes an introduction to the field of science to which its pioneers contributed, line illustrations, photographs, a glossary of scientific terms related to the research described in the text, and a listing of further resources for information about the general subject matter.

The goal of this set is to provide, at an appropriate level, factual information about pioneering scientists. The authors hope that readers will be inspired to achieve greatness themselves, to feel connected to the people behind science, and to believe that they may have a positive and enduring impact on society.

ACKNOWLEDGMENTS

I would like to thank Frank K. Darmstadt, Executive Editor of science and mathematics at Infobase Publishing, for his skillful guidance and extreme patience, and to Melissa Cullen-DuPont, for having all the answers. Appreciation is also extended to illustrator Bobbi McCutcheon for her dedicated professionalism and to Ann E. Hicks for her constructive suggestions. The reference librarians and support staff of the main branch of the Medina County District Library, located in Medina, Ohio, deserve acknowledgment for their assistance in obtaining interlibrary loans, acquiring numerous special requests, and handling the hundreds of materials and resources the author borrowed during the writing of this set. Gratitude is also expressed to Pam Shirk, former media specialist at A. I. Root Middle School in Medina, Ohio, for sharing her expertise. Many people and organizations generously gave permission to use their photographs. Their names are acknowledged underneath the donated images. Thank you all.

INTRODUCTION

The first exposure of many scientists to the natural sciences is through biology, broadly defined as the study of life. They may have enjoyed collecting bugs as children or helped grow vegetables in their mothers' gardens. Perhaps they pressed wildflowers into wax paper as young scouts or watched in awe as family dogs gave birth to litters of puppies. Because people are living beings, learning about life may have felt comfortable. Most high schools require students to take a biology course, during which they study the major human organ systems, and it seems fairly easy to comprehend —all creatures, including human beings, need to breathe, take in food, and reproduce. Understanding biology at a deeper level, however, requires more than memorizing the names of the 206 bones of the human body. Biologists must grasp the basics of chemistry, since organisms ultimately are composed of the elements carbon, oxygen, hydrogen, and nitrogen. They must be cognizant of the physical laws that govern our development and movement. Knowledge of the environment is also crucial to become a successful biologist, as organisms are integral components of the ecosystems in which they live.

For hundreds of years, the subject of biology consisted of two main branches: botany, the study of plants, and zoology, the study of animals. Modern restructuring of the subject matter of biology led to a hierarchical system for ordering life. By initially focusing on the organism, one can either look inward or outward. Looking inward, an organism may be reduced to a collection of physiological systems, which can be reduced further to organs, and then tissues, cells, and molecules. By this approach organisms are merely a complex construction of chemical elements. Progressing in the other direction, one must recognize that organisms are integral components of a multifarious ecological network. They often live in groups called demes within larger geographical populations of their species, anatomically similar individuals capable of inter-breeding. Each species occupies a unique niche or role within the biological *community* of an *ecosystem*. The biosphere refers to the global ecosystem that encompasses all of Earth's ecosystems and ranges from high in the atmosphere down to the ocean depths and below the ground.

While all branches of biology are interested in the fundamentals of life, different fields view life from different perspectives. Each hierarchical level builds upon the foundation knowledge of the preceding one, beginning with cellular and molecular biology. The cell is the smallest structural unit of life that can function independently. Cells themselves are constructed of large biological molecules including proteins, carbohydrates, lipids, and nucleic acids. The study of the structure and function of molecules responsible for life is called molecular biology, and the study of life at the cellular level is cell biology. Though the English scientist Robert Hooke discovered cells in the 17th century, the fact that all living things were composed of cells was not recognized until 1839, when the German biologist Theodor Schwann proposed the cell theory based on his own research and that of Matthias Schleiden. Today cell biologists universally accept cells as the basic unit of life and explore phenomena such as the control of cell division and the regulation of molecular traffic across the cell membrane. Molecular biology originated in the middle of the 20th century, when technological advances allowed scientists to elucidate the molecular structures of proteins and nucleic acids. Molecular biologists examine processes such as the mutation of DNA by carcinogenic chemicals and the modification of proteins in response to a hormone binding to its specific receptor.

At the organismal level, the specific subject under scrutiny often names disciplines. To list a few, a protozoologist studies protists, a herpetologist studies reptiles and amphibians, and a mycologist studies fungi. Within each discipline different subdisciplines describe an area of focus. For example, a physiologist studies how different parts of an organism cooperate to achieve a functional goal such as gas exchange, nitrogenous waste excretion, or nutrient absorption. She might investigate how the gills and kidneys of a marine fish work together to compensate for the loss of water from osmosis. An anatomist, one who studies the structure of living things, might compare the hearts of different vertebrates, noting the existence of two-, three-, and four-chambered hearts in different classes. An embryologist studies the early development of plants and animals.

Ecology is the study of the relationships among organisms and their environments, including biotic (living) factors and abiotic (nonliving) factors. A greater awareness about the connection between the health of the Earth and its inhabitants led to an increase in the amount of ecological research scientists performed throughout the 20th century. Population ecology is concerned with the interactions and activities of groups of organisms that live within the same area at the same time. A researcher might examine how competition for a limited food resource controls the size of a population. At the community level, an ecologist considers all the populations of species that live in a geographic area. She might examine which grasses and wildflowers initially repopulate a community after a fire ravages a forest. A system ecologist is concerned with ecosystems, consisting of several populations of organisms and the physical environment in which they live. He might study the cause of recurrent algal blooms in a freshwater lake, a condition that occurs when the normally present algal forms overgrow and deplete the water of oxygen, on which the fish and aquatic invertebrates depend.

Even though hierarchical levels provide a solid structural frame for organizing life, many branches of biology span multiple levels. A biologist can study genetics from the molecular level or by examining trends in a population. A molecular geneticist might research the mutations in a sequence of DNA that result in a white flower rather than a purple flower, while a population geneticist might be interested in the different allele frequencies for two populations of plants growing on nearby islands. An evolutionist might be interested in the origin of membrane-bound organelles or the divergence of two species arriving at different anatomical solutions for the same physiological problem. A biologist who researches a phenomenon in which bacteria help a leguminous plant synthesize nitrogen might call herself a botanist, a microbiologist, an ecologist, or even a biochemist!

Regardless of his or her preference for various classification schemes or areas of research, a biologist is certain to encounter themes common to all branches and fields. The principle that structure determines function pervades all levels and disciplines of the biological sciences. At the subcellular level, the stacking of membrane-bound thylakoids inside a chloroplast increases the membrane surface area that holds the light-harvesting photosystems necessary for carrying out photosynthesis. At the organismal level, the sleek body shape of a shark allows it to glide through the water with minimal energy input. An evolutionary theme also permeates the biological sciences: all living organisms are related to one another. Though some may find it offensive that human beings evolved from the same common ancestor as a sea cucumber or a slime mold, the fact is that all organisms share a universal genetic code, meaning the same three nucleotides encode the same amino acid in a thermophilic Archaean and in a sparrow.

This volume in the Pioneers in Science set profiles 10 individuals who contributed to the development of modern biology in different ways. Opening up a new line of research distinguishes some of the scientists; the obstacles overcome to move a field forward distinguish others. William Harvey was a 17th-century English physician who demonstrated that blood circulated throughout the body, pumped by the muscular heart, thereby disproving an authority on anatomy who was undisputed for 1,400 years. A Dutch draper named Antoni van Leeuwenhoek had no scientific training but instructed the members of the world's most prominent scientific society about microscopic life. As the number of species known to humans increased exponentially, the organizational genius of

Swedish botanist Carl Linnaeus made possible more efficient communication among naturalists by the development of binomial nomenclature. The most famous evolutionist of all time, English naturalist Charles Darwin, proposed natural selection as the mechanism for the evolution of species, which was likely the most controversial theory of all time. In an Augustinian monastery in the 1800s, Gregor Mendel bred thousands of pea plants, dutifully recorded his observations on thousands of offspring, and used mathematical analysis to solve the mysteries of inheritance. Another geneticist, an American, Thomas Hunt Morgan, demonstrated the physical nature of genes and described sex-linked inheritance. Without the support of an academic research institution, funds, or suitable equipment, the entomologist and animal behaviorist Charles Henry Turner demonstrated that insects could hear and learn. The Scottish bacteriologist Sir Alexander Fleming serendipitously discovered that the mold *Penicillium* produced a miraculous chemical substance that killed bacterial pathogens. The Italian-American researcher Rita Levi-Montalcini began her research career by performing dissections on chicken eggs in a secret lab with homemade equipment and tools and went on to discover the first growth factor, leading to a revolution in cell biology and medicine. James Watson, an American postdoctoral student floundering in his career, solved the double helical structure of DNA by tinkering with pieces of wire and cardboard. Though their accomplishments vary in scope and their discoveries represent a variety of subfields in biology, all of the aforementioned biologists are worthy of the title "Pioneer in Science."

William Harvey

1

(1578–1657)

William Harvey is considered the father of modern physiology. (*Library of Congress, Prints and Photographs Division [LC-USZ62-128713]*)

On the Circulation of Blood throughout the Body

Physicians did not know much about the workings of the human body 400 years ago. Physicians thought a person's physical and psychological health were governed by the balance of four body fluids called humors: *blood*, phlegm, yellow bile, and black bile. If the quantities of these humors were off balance, one fell ill, and a diagnosis was dependent on the physician determining which humor was affected based on the patient's symptoms. To treat the illnesses, the physician would do whatever was necessary to force out the excess humor of the affected system. While medical training today includes the mastery of human *anatomy* through performing detailed cadaver *dissections*, such procedures were considered sacrilegious mutilations until the late 17th century. Physicians relied on the teachings of the early Greek physician Claudius Galen (about 129–200 C.E.) in order to diagnose and treat illnesses. Galen was considered the authority on human anatomy, and his theories went virtually unquestioned for almost 1,400 years. Because learning about human anatomy was limited to examinations of the human body's exterior, Galen dissected apes and made conclusions about internal human anatomy from those observations. Physicians did not begin to doubt Galenic teaching until the 17th century. A bold man named William Harvey definitively disproved Galen's theories about the blood and the *heart*. He discovered that blood circulates throughout the body, pumped by the muscular heart.

From Folkestone Farmboy to London Physician

William Harvey was born on April 1, 1578, in the small coastal town of Folkestone, England. He was the eldest of seven sons. Thomas Harvey and his second wife, Joan Halke, also had two daughters. Harvey senior was a farmer and a landowner and later in life became a successful businessman. While not much is known about William's early childhood years, it is certain that while helping out on his father's farm he became interested in how the body was built and functioned. He reportedly dissected small animals in his mother's kitchen as a child. When William was 10 years old, he attended the King's School in Canterbury. He received a scholarship to study arts and medicine at Gonville and Caius College at Cambridge University and obtained his bachelor's degree in 1597.

In 1602, Harvey received a doctorate of medicine from the University of Padua in Italy, the most reputable medical school at the time. Most of the anatomy Harvey was taught at Padua stemmed from the teachings of Aristotle and Galen. Galen was extremely prolific on the topic of anatomy, yet most of his writings were based on animal observations since human dissections were prohibited in his day. Because his doctrines were consistent with Christian theology, which was becoming popularized, Galen's works and reputation were well protected for 1,500 years. Most physicians still relied on his teachings, though a few dared to begin questioning some of his assertions.

After obtaining his medical degree, Harvey set up a private practice in London. He obtained his full licensure to practice medicine, and he began to acquire many famous patients. In 1604, he married Elizabeth Browne, the daughter of one of King James I's many physicians. They had a happy marriage but never had any children. Harvey was elected to membership in the Royal College of Physicians in 1607 and two years later was appointed physician to St. Bartholomew's Hospital, one of two hospitals that treated poor patients. This position required him to visit the hospital about once each week, examine some of the patients, and direct the staff of three surgeons, one *apothecary*, and 13 nurses. From 1615 to 1656, he was the Lumleian lecturer of surgery for the Royal College and gave lectures about anatomy. In 1618, he replaced his father-in-law as one of the king's physicians, a position he continued to hold when King Charles's reign began in 1625. Harvey became a close companion of King Charles and was loyal to him even during and after the Cromwellian civil war.

Galen's Authority Questioned

In order to appreciate the contribution that Harvey made to modern anatomy, one must first understand what was then accepted as true concerning the *circulatory system*. Aristotle had proposed that the liver made the blood, which was carried through the body in the *veins* and was cooled by the brain. He also believed that the heart was the body's main organ and was responsible for emotions and intelligence. Galen expanded these ideas into the belief that the body was organized into three separate physiological systems. The main organ of the first system was the liver, which made the dark blood from food cooked in the stomach. These "natural spirits" were then carried around the body by the veins, and blood was absorbed by the different body parts as needed. The main organ of the second system was the heart, the so-called seat of the soul that served as an innate source of heat for the body. The heart was also responsible for preparing the life-giving "vital spirits" by mixing the blood with air from the lungs, a process that also acted to cool the heart. After being mixed with air, the bright red blood then would be carried throughout the body via the arteries. Lastly, the brain served as a source of "animal spirits" that were responsible for sensation and motion and were distributed throughout the body through hollow nerve tubes. Galen noted that blood moved from the right side of the heart to the left and suggested it was moving through tiny pores or openings in the *septum*, the wall that separates the two sides of the heart. The blood was thought to move through the body by a force contained within the spirits themselves. Because these ideas were sanctioned by the church, Galen's ideas went unchallenged for centuries.

Flemish anatomist and physician Andreas Vesalius was the first to question Galen publicly. He noticed that Galen's observations and anatomical descriptions about humans must have been made from observations of monkeys and apes. Vesalius was a member of the faculty at the University of Padua in the early 16th century and bravely used human dissections as part of his anatomy lectures. Based on his own observations, he proposed that Galen never even dissected a human and proceeded to publish the most accurate textbook on human anatomy to that date. In 1559, one of Vesalius's students, Realdo Columbo, wrote *On Anatomy*, in which he stated that blood did not move through pores within the septum, but from the right side of the heart to the left via the lungs. Resistant to new ideas, the medical faculty at Padua continued to follow Galenic tradition. Girolamo Fabrici, more commonly known as Fabricius, was one of Harvey's teachers. In 1603, he discovered that veins contained structures that looked like little flaps. He called these *valves* and suggested their purpose was to control the amount of blood sent to certain body parts. They prevented blood from collecting in the lower body parts. Fabricius was devoted to Galen, however, and did not extend the observations any further.

This was the doctrine of the early 17th century, when Harvey became bothered by the disagreement between what he was taught and what he observed on his own. From his Lumleian lecture notes scholars learned that Harvey began formulating his opinions on the heart and blood before 1616. However, it was not until he published a 68-page booklet titled *On the Motion of the Heart and Blood in Animals* in 1628 that the world finally, though still reluctantly, began to consider the Galenic doctrines more critically. Within a few decades physicians widely accepted Harvey's discoveries.

Blood Circulation

The overwhelming conclusion that revolutionized thought concerning the heart and blood was that blood circulated through the body. That is, the same blood passed through the veins, heart, and arteries over and over, hence the current nomenclature, the "circulatory system." Ignoring such nonsense as spirits and mysterious forces, Harvey determined that the heart was simply a muscle, a mechanical pump that alternately contracted and relaxed with each beat. He compared its action to blowing air into a surgical glove. As air fills the glove, the glove expands. Then the heart contracts, and in doing so, its chambers shrink. Blood is expelled into the arteries, which makes them pulse or temporarily bulge. This action sends the blood traveling throughout the body. The veins carry blood in a single direction back to the heart. Reverse flow in the veins is prevented by the action of valves, discovered by his professor Fabricius. Similar valves are found between the atria and the ventricles in the heart. These valves prevent blood from returning to the atria after moving to the ventricles and into the arteries.

Today, the pathway of blood circulation is commonly known. Blood enters the right atrium of the heart through the vena cava, then passes through a valve into the right ventricle. Blood travels from the right ventricle to the lungs via the pulmonary *artery*. Oxygenated blood returns to the heart through the pulmonary vein at the left atrium and moves through another valve into the left ventricle, the strongest chamber of the heart. The left ventricle pumps the blood into the aorta, which carries the freshly oxygenated blood to all the body parts. Within the body tissues the arteries empty into *capillaries*, which connect to veins and eventually dump their now deoxygenated blood into the vena cava.

Harvey had performed many dissections and *vivisections* (dissections performed on living animals), and he presented several types

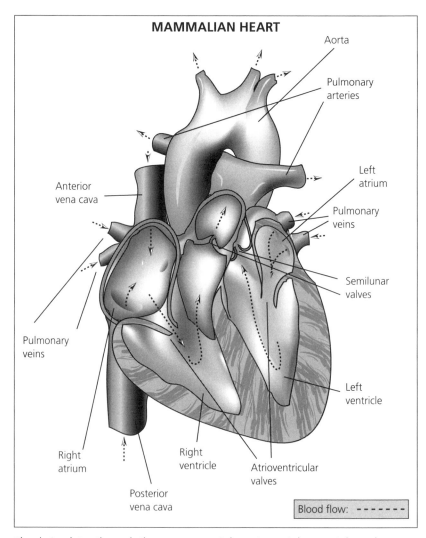

MAMMALIAN HEART

Aorta

Pulmonary arteries

Left atrium

Anterior vena cava

Pulmonary veins

Semilunar valves

Pulmonary veins

Left ventricle

Right atrium

Right ventricle

Atrioventricular valves

Posterior vena cava

Blood flow: - - - - - - -

Blood circulates through the vena cava, right atrium, right ventricle, pulmonary arteries, lungs, pulmonary veins, left atrium, left ventricle, aorta, arteries, body tissues, veins, and back to the vena cava.

of evidence in defense of his revolutionary statements. He crudely measured the amount of blood the heart pumps with each contraction. Using this estimate, he calculated that in a single hour the heart pumps a quantity of blood three times the weight of an average man. It was difficult to fathom the liver producing this much blood and the body parts absorbing as much. The same blood must flow continuously throughout the arteries and veins. He described several experiments that confirmed his conclusions. For example, he tied off the vena cava of a living snake. The result was the heart becoming pale and emptying of blood. When the aorta was tied off, the heart filled with blood that could not escape. If he tightly tied a cloth around a man's upper arm, the deep arterial blood flow was blocked, the arm became pale, and a bulge appeared on the heart side of the cloth. If the cloth was loosened, arterial flow brought blood down the arm, but the blood could not return through the more superficial veins, and as a result the arm turned purplish and bulged. Harvey also detailed the anatomical evidence based on the structure and orientation of the valves within the veins and within the heart. He was able to insert probes through the little doorways only in one direction, the same direction that leads to the heart. If he probed through the valves in the other direction, they were functionally destroyed.

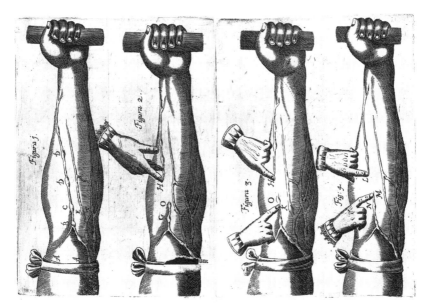

To demonstrate that blood flowed from the heart in a unidirectional manner, Harvey tied a restrictive band around the upper arm and pressed on the blood vessels in the lower arm at various points. (*Library of Congress, Prints and Photographs Division [LC-USZ62-95251]*)

Harvey did not mention the purpose of blood circulation. Today physiologists know that the circulatory system is responsible for transporting all materials into and out of body tissues. Oxygen necessary for metabolism is picked up from the lungs by pulmonary circulation and sent to all parts of the body. At the body tissues, waste products of metabolism such as carbon dioxide are carried away from the body tissues through the veins and eventually expelled through the lungs. Blood also carries sugars and amino acids for anabolic purposes to all parts of the body as well as hormones that allow communication among body parts. Harvey was unaware of capillaries, tiny vessels that connect arteries to veins within the tissues. These structures were discovered by the Italian physician Marcello Malpighi with the assistance of a microscope.

Malpighi's Discovery of Capillaries

Italian physician and anatomist Marcello Malpighi (1628–94) was one of the first scientists to study anatomy at the microscopic level. He made many discoveries, and as a result, many anatomical structures are named in his honor—Malpighian corpuscles of the circulatory system, Malpighian layer of the skin, and Malpighian tubes of insects. Considered the father of *histology*, the microscopic study of tissues, Malpighi carefully examined and described tissues of the spinal cord, brain, kidneys, spleen, skin, and tongue. He also made substantial contributions to the field of developmental biology by presenting detailed descriptions of developing insect *larvae* and animal embryos. Four years after Harvey's death, Malpighi discovered factual evidence that substantiated the theory of blood circulation that Harvey had proposed in 1628. Though many ridiculed Harvey for suggesting blood circulated throughout the body, Malpighi's discovery of capillaries proved Harvey was correct.

Believing in the divine rule of kings, King Charles abolished Parliament in 1629. In 1642, civil war broke out between King Charles's supporters and Parliament's supporters. Harvey's research papers were all destroyed when the living quarters of the king's palace were ransacked. By 1639, Harvey had been promoted to chief physician of King Charles. In return for Harvey's loyalty, the king supported his research by providing him with deer from the Royal Parks, which Harvey used for dissections. When Harvey followed the king to Oxford, Harvey was given the position of warden for Merton College at Oxford University as a favor by the king. In 1646, the king surrendered himself to Parliament and was eventually beheaded in 1649.

In 1649, Harvey responded publicly for the first time to criticism, and especially to the French doctor Jean Riolan, of his *On the*

Malpighi had been examining lung tissue from frogs under the microscope in 1661, when he observed the small tubes. This demonstrated that blood did not pour out of the blood vessels, but remained enclosed. He concluded that capillaries connected arteries and veins, completing the circulation of blood.

The circulatory system is composed of a closed network of tubes that transport the blood that is pumped through the vessels by the heart. Arteries carry the blood away from the heart, and veins return the blood to the heart. Larger arteries branch into smaller arterioles, which lead to capillaries, the tiny vessels that connect arteries to veins. Capillaries are extremely thin, allowing gases and other *molecules* to easily diffuse through their walls. Oxygen and nutrients pass into the body tissues where they are utilized. Metabolic waste products such as carbon dioxide diffuse into the capillaries, which then converge into slightly larger vessels called venules. The venules lead to veins, which carry the waste materials away from the body's tissues. Because oxygen gives blood its red color, oxygen-rich arterial blood appears red. As the blood reaches the capillaries, the oxygen diffuses into the body tissues. Thus, by the time it reaches the veins, it has lost its red color and appears blue.

Motion treatise. Harvey not only responded but also provided additional evidence supporting his original claims. Around this time, the criticism began to die down as his work was accepted by the newer generation of physicians.

Reproduction and Embryology

While Harvey's discoveries regarding blood circulation advanced the field of *physiology* immeasurably and rendered him famous, he was also interested in animal reproduction. While at Merton, one professor allowed Harvey access to his hens, and Harvey spent much time there examining the eggs. In 1651, he published *On the Reproduction of Animals*. While this treatise was not nearly as controversial as his publication *On the Motion*, it earned Harvey recognition for presenting the most accurate and well-documented day-to-day development of the chick.

Harvey wondered about the generation of life and what each parent contributed to an embryo. There had been many suggestions through the years. One idea, *preformation*, suggested that an entire miniature organism was already present within each egg. At birth, each female has eggs that contain entire beings already inside them, which also contain even smaller entire beings already inside them, and so on. This belief was endorsed by the church. Other physicians believed that semen mixed with menstrual blood to form an embryo. In his text, Harvey stated that all animals, including mammals, arise from eggs, a doctrine called the "primacy of the egg." His beliefs that led up to this statement were actually incorrect. However, his publication did shift the focus of reproduction to eggs, which eventually led to the appreciation of both the egg and sperm in the reproduction of animals.

Father of Modern Physiology

William Harvey remained an active member of the Royal College of Physicians over the years. When his duties as a royal physician became too time-consuming to actively participate in the business of the college, he donated money to build a library, pay a librarian, and fund an annual lecture. He was offered the position of president in 1654 but declined due to advanced age. On June 3, 1657, in Roehampton, London, Harvey suffered a fatal stroke and was buried in the family vault at Hempstead Church in Essex.

Harvey's discovery of blood circulation was a tremendous jump forward for the field of medicine. His method of making careful observations and drawing conclusions based only on the findings was a revolutionary new approach that paved the way for modern physiology. Before Harvey, physicians relied heavily on the texts of ancient philosophers in order to understand the workings of the human body. The writings were based on conjecture and feeble analysis and thus delayed the advancement of medical knowledge for centuries. Harvey demonstrated the importance of discovery by direct observation and exploration rather than reading alone. He was a quiet, conservative man, and it took a lot of courage for him to speak against the millennium-old Galenic tradition. Even so, his meticulous methodology gave him the confidence to question the recognized authority. Because he taught others to accept only that which could be observed and thus removed the long-standing obstacle to further progress, Harvey is considered the father of modern physiology.

CHRONOLOGY

1578	William Harvey is born on April 1 in Folkestone, England
1593	Attends Gonville and Caius College, Cambridge University
1597	Receives bachelor's degree from Caius College, Cambridge University
1600	Attends the University of Padua in Italy
1602	Receives doctor of medicine degree from Padua
1604	Becomes licensed to practice medicine in London
1607	Is elected a fellow of the Royal College of Physicians
1609	Is appointed physician at St. Bartholomew's Hospital in London

1615—43 Is a professor at St. Bartholomew's Hospital

1616—56 Royal College of Physicians names Harvey the Lumleian lecturer of surgery

1618 Replaces father-in-law as one of King James I's doctors

1625 Becomes a royal physician for King Charles I

1628 Publishes *On the Motion of the Heart and Blood in Animals,* which summarized his revolutionary ideas including the theory that blood circulates throughout the body

1630 Becomes one of King Charles I's regular doctors

1639 Becomes one of King Charles I's chief doctors

1642 Harvey's papers and notes are destroyed during the English Civil War

1645 Becomes warden of Merton College, Oxford, and starts studying chicken development

1648 Publicly responds to criticism

1651 Publishes *On the Reproduction of Animals,* introducing primacy of the egg doctrine

1657 Dies following a stroke on June 3 in Roehampton, London

FURTHER READING

Allaby, Michael, and Derek Gjertsen, eds. *Makers of Science.* Vol. 1. New York: Oxford University Press, 2002. Chronological biographies of influential scientists. Includes political and social settings as well as scientific achievements.

French, Roger. *William Harvey's Natural Philosophy.* Cambridge: Cambridge University Press, 1994. Extensive discussion of Harvey's methods of discovery and the 17th-century reactions to his views.

Gillispie, Charles C., ed. *Dictionary of Scientific Biography.* Vol. 6. New York: Scribner, 1970–76. Good source for facts concerning personal backgrounds and scientific accomplishments but assumes reader has basic knowledge of science.

Porter, Roy. "About William Harvey." The William Harvey Medical Research Foundation, 1998. Available online. URL: http://www.williamharvey.org/wm_harvey.htm. Accessed on January 12, 2005. Information about Harvey's discoveries, quotes from his original writings, and links to information about the foundation that bears his name.

Scientists and Inventors. New York: Macmillan Library Reference, 1998. Brief profiles of the life and works of more than 100 notable scientists. Written for middle and high school students.

Spangenburg, Ray, and Diane K. Moser. *The Birth of Science: Ancient Times to 1699.* New York: Facts On File, 2004. Outlines the history of science, building on the ideas of great minds and of their predecessors. Intended for middle and high school students.

2

Antoni van Leeuwenhoek

(1632–1723)

Antoni van Leeuwenhoek is considered the father of protozoology and bacteriology. (*Biophoto Associates/Photo Researchers, Inc.*)

Discovery of Microscopic Life

Humans seem small and insignificant when considering the vastness of our universe. The 6-billion-plus population of humans on the entire Earth is dwarfed by the number of *bacteria* that can grow in a single glass flask of nutrient *broth* overnight in a laboratory incubator. Millions of *microorganisms* can fit into a single drop of water; perhaps our entire seemingly enormous universe can fit on the head of a pin in some other being's universe. All size is relative.

When microorganisms were first observed in the 17th century by a Dutch cloth merchant named Antoni (pronounced An-TON-ee) van Leeuwenhoek (pronounced LAY-when-hook), a new world was discovered. Because of his discovery Leeuwenhoek is regarded as the father of the fields of *bacteriology* and *protozoology*. The Earth has nurtured these tiny life forms for more than 3 billion years. They constantly surround us, living in the air, in the water, and on dry land. They are present in our homes, in our food, and on our bodies, yet humans have been aware of their existence for only a little more than 300 years. Imagine society's shock when it learned of Leeuwenhoek's findings.

Son of a Basket Maker

Antoni van Leeuwenhoek was the fifth child, but the first son, of Philips van Leeuwenhoek and Margaretha Bel van den Berch. He was born on October 24, 1632, in Delft, Holland. Delft was a clean, pleasant village with lots of canals and was well known for beer making. Philips was a basket maker, as was his father before him. The Leeuwenhoeks had one more son and one more daughter after Antoni. Antoni's father died in 1638, and three years later his mother remarried to a painter, who died when Antoni was 16 years old.

When he was about eight, Antoni was sent to grammar school 20 miles (32 km) from home at Warmond. Afterward he lived temporarily with an uncle who was both an attorney and a town clerk at Benthuizen, located about nine miles (14.5 km) from Delft. When he reached the age of 16, Antoni was sent to Amsterdam to serve as an apprentice to a linen draper. He was a diligent, responsible worker and served as cashier and bookkeeper as well. In 1654, Antoni returned to Delft, where he spent the rest of his life.

Leeuwenhoek wed Barbara de Mey shortly after his return to Delft. He was 21, and she was 24 years old. He bought a house and opened his own draper business. The Leeuwenhoeks eventually had three sons and two daughters, all of whom died in infancy except Maria, who was born in 1656. Barbara died in 1666, leaving Leeuwenhoek alone after 12 years of marriage. In 1671, he married Cornelia Swalmius, a relative of Barbara's.

Leeuwenhoek's business was successful, and he spent most of his days inspecting fabrics and selling cloth, buttons, and ribbon. He was also employed as chamberlain to the sheriffs of Delft from 1660 to 1699. In addition, he was appointed surveyor to the court of Holland from 1669 until his death and was a wine gauger from 1679 onward. He gained a favorable reputation among the inhabitants of his quaint Dutch town, and he secured enough money to support his scientific hobbies.

A Skilled Lens Grinder

While it is not known exactly when Leeuwenhoek became preoccupied with microscopy of biological specimens, it is certain that it was before 1673, when the first preserved correspondence concerning his microscopic examinations appeared. In the 17th century, grinding lenses for magnifying glasses was a skill not uncommon to drapers. After all, cloth merchants had to inspect the weave of their linens carefully. Leeuwenhoek developed an especially remarkable talent in this area and reportedly constructed about 550 lenses during his lifetime.

After carefully grinding a lens with a gritty material, he polished it with a fine-grained putty and mounted it between two brass plates that had openings specially designed to hold the tiny lens, which was less than one-eighth of an inch wide. A series of pins with screws at one end were also attached to the brass plates in order to move and hold the object in position in front of the lens. Leeuwenhoek usually left specimens fixed to his microscopes so he could continue to view them whenever he pleased. Compound microscopes, those using more than one lens, were also in use at the time. Though the possible *magnification* with compound microscopes was larger than with simple microscopes, the images were often blurred or the colors distorted. Leeuwenhoek started examining objects other than cloth products with his lenses, inspecting anything he suspected might be interesting when magnified. Most of his specimens were biological. For example, he observed insect wings and eyes, *pollen* grains, and *mold*.

A friend of Leeuwenhoek's from Delft, Dutch physician Regnier de Graaf, had seen Leeuwenhoek's work. He thought Leeuwenhoek's microscopes were finer than the best ones used by acad-

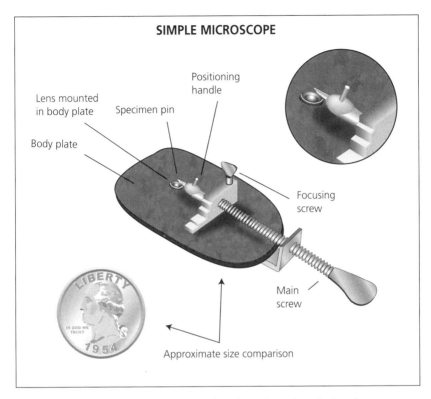

SIMPLE MICROSCOPE

Positioning handle

Lens mounted in body plate

Specimen pin

Body plate

Focusing screw

Main screw

Approximate size comparison

LIBERTY

IN GOD WE TRUST

1954

The microscopes that Leeuwenhoek crafted fit in the palm of a hand.

emicians at the time. He asked Leeuwenhoek to record some of his investigations. After composing his own plea for England's Royal Society to consider Leeuwenhoek's recorded observations, de Graaf mailed Leeuwenhoek's notes to England's most prestigious academic organization. Leeuwenhoek's notes consisted of descriptions of fungal spores, a common louse, and the stinger, mouth, and eye of a bee. This correspondence was published in the *Philosophical Transactions of the Royal Society* in 1673.

Like de Graaf, the fellows of the Royal Society were impressed and wanted to hear more from the Dutch draper. Leeuwenhoek humbly responded with more detailed notes and observations as well as illustrations prepared by a draughtsman based on Leeuwenhoek's sketches. In this second letter, Leeuwenhoek also admitted to being uneducated in any language but his native tongue, Dutch. This was very unusual for a scientist at the time since most scientific correspondence was in Latin, English, or French. Furthermore, Leeuwenhoek was not familiar with scientific writing, which is usually clear and concise. His letters were long, rambling, and often included bits of personal information. Some members possibly were repulsed by this crude, uneducated man. It is just as likely that some were amused by his straightforward, unashamed manner. Most were impressed, however, as Leeuwenhoek's correspondence with the Royal Society of London continued for 50 years until his death.

Animalcules

Leeuwenhoek's most famous communication transpired in the year 1676. He claimed that he saw tiny living "animalcules" swimming

Prokaryotes and Eukaryotes

When Leeuwenhoek first examined pond water under a microscope, he probably saw a combination of both eukaryotic and *prokaryotic* organisms. Microorganisms include all organisms that are too small to be seen with the unaided eye, but that leaves a lot of room for variability. The most prominent difference between the two types is that the *cells* of prokaryotic organisms do not possess membrane-bound organelles. Eukaryotic organisms are made of cells that have membrane-enclosed organelles and possess a higher level of internal organization than do prokaryotic organisms.

Prokaryotes are single-celled organisms that range in size from 5×10^{-6} inches (125 nm) to a 50th of an inch (about 500 μm) in length. Technically, some are large enough to be seen without a microscope, but the overwhelming majority are closer to 4×10^{-5} inches (1 μm) in length. The basic shape of prokaryotic cells is either a rod or spherical, but several variations also exist, including spiral-shaped. Though one cell makes up an entire organism, several individual cells may form special arrange-

about in rainwater, and he estimated that 1,000 of these tiny creatures could fit on the head of a pin. Anyone who had been ignoring his previous claims was paying attention now! Leeuwenhoek explained how in 1674 he had visited a lake a few hours from Delft and taken samples of the water, which he described as murky and covered with green clouds. He was amazed to see many types of tiny creatures rapidly moving in the liquid. After this discovery, he started looking for these animalcules in other locations. He examined samples of snow, rain, seawater, and well water. They were everywhere. He finally wrote a long letter giving very vivid descriptions of the little animals, which we now know were mostly *protozoa*, microscopic, unicellular, *eukaryotic* (containing a nucleus and other membrane-bound organelles) organisms. The colors ranged from green to clear. The organisms

ments such as clusters or chains. Other characteristics, such as nutritional requirements, means of motility, and ecological impact, exhibit a wide degree of diversity. The prokaryotic kingdom consists of two entire domains of life forms, the Archaea and the Bacteria. These two domains are distinguished by unique nucleic acid sequences, composition of the *cell wall,* and types of chemical bonds found in the membrane lipids. Though not as visible to humans, the prokaryotes of the world outnumber the *eukaryotes* by several orders of magnitude.

Eukaryotes may be either single-celled or multicellular organisms. While most animals and plants are large enough to be seen without assistance, other eukaryotes are considered microorganisms. Eukaryotic microorganisms include fungi such as molds and yeasts and protists such as algae, euglena, and amoeba. Though all eukaryotes possess membrane-bound organelles, the extent and variety of organelle types differ among *species.* For example, only organisms that undergo photosynthesis to obtain energy possess chloroplasts, the specially designed structures capable of carrying out this process. As determined by his notes and diagrams, the animalcules Leeuwenhoek first observed were mostly protists, the most diverse of all the eukaryotes. Since his discovery more than 60,000 protist species have been identified.

were a variety of shapes including round, oval, and even spiral. Some had what he described as fins or legs or little hairs. The "wretched beasties" swam around quickly using different types of motion.

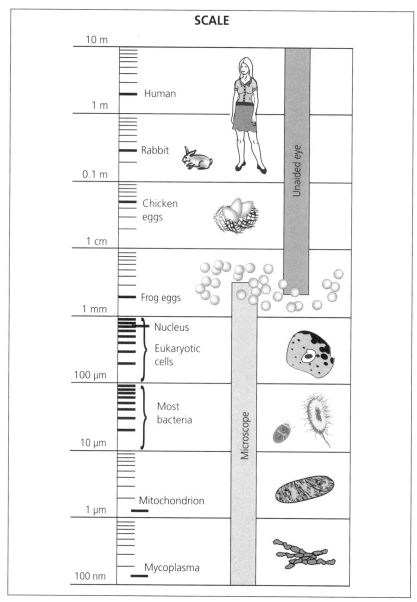

SCALE

10 m

1 m — Human

Rabbit

0.1 m

Chicken eggs

1 cm

Frog eggs

1 mm

Nucleus

Eukaryotic cells

100 μm

Most bacteria

10 μm

Mitochondrion

1 μm

Mycoplasma

100 nm

Unaided eye

Microscope

With his skillfully crafted microscopes, Leeuwenhoek was able to observe clearly microorganisms as small as one micron.

Microscopes had been around for approximately 50 years when Leeuwenhoek began his studies. He was by no means the inventor of the microscope, yet he was able to obtain clear images of magnifications more than 250 times the original size. Not only was he able to achieve great magnifications, but they were viewed with good *resolution*. Resolution, or resolving power, is the ability to distinguish fine detail. Leeuwenhoek was able to achieve resolutions of approximately 1 μm. Some of the people who read the communications from him to the Royal Society thought it impossible that such great magnifications could be reached with only a single lens. In order to magnify things, lenses must be convex in shape, meaning rounded out. Leeuwenhoek's lenses were so convex they were practically spherical. He never taught anyone how he achieved such remarkable results with his lenses nor let anyone watch him make them, so it is understandable that some doubted his claims, especially now that he was proclaiming that the world was filled with wretched beasties that were invisible to the naked eyes. He was labeled everything from a liar to a magician, but he was merely a skilled observer driven by his natural curiosity to understand the world around him.

To respond to the doubters, Leeuwenhoek provided affidavits from eight reputable men including clergymen, attorneys, and physicians. But when the Royal Society examined specimens similar to the ones in which Leeuwenhoek said he had found the tiny creatures, they saw nothing. Finally, they asked fellow Robert Hooke to repeat exactly Leeuwenhoek's procedures. Hooke was the society's curator of experiments and was considered an expert microscopist. In 1665, he had published a text titled *Micrographia*, which included drawings and descriptions of enlarged, detailed sections of insects, fossils, cloth, and mold. Hooke also was the first to report the existence of cells in cork (from tree bark). Cells are the basic structural and functional unit of life. They make up the tissues of our bodies, reproduce themselves, and perform all the functions necessary to support life, such as respiration, excretion, and building of *proteins*. Since *Micrographia* was not written in Dutch, Leeuwenhoek could not have read it, but he could have looked at the pictures or been told about the contents by others. This may have been his initial inspiration for examining objects other than fabrics. When Hooke repeated Leeuwenhoek's experiments and published that he was able to see minuscule swimming creatures in 1678, the academic establishment replaced their doubts with amazement for this newly discovered living world.

Pepper and Fame

Whenever he was curious about something, Leeuwenhoek sought answers through exploration with his microscopes. For example, he wondered what gave pepper its characteristic biting flavor; perhaps the pepper grains were covered with bunches of tiny sharp points. He softened pepper by soaking it in water, and then he sucked the samples into tiny cylindrical glass tubes for viewing. He was astonished to find not only the animalcules that he had seen in the past, but hundreds of thousands of creatures even smaller than the previously admired protists. He estimated that 100 of them aligned end to end would not attain the width of a grain of sand. He wrote up these findings to Hooke in 1678. This correspondence began a series of papers considered to be the first in bacteriology. Bacteria are unicellular, prokaryotic (containing no nucleus) organisms that approximate 4×10^{-5} inches (1 μm) in size.

In 1680, Leeuwenhoek was elected a full fellow of the Royal Society. While he never went to the meetings in London, he wrote more than 200 letters to the society. Some biographers report more, but it is likely that some of these are simply translations of the original Dutch letters. Most of these were published in the *Philosophical Transactions of the Royal Society* over the next several decades. In 1699, he was nominated a corresponding member of the Académie des Sciences of Paris. He was known all over the world and had frequent visitors. The queen of England and the emperor of Germany were among the numerous foreign dignitaries who visited him. In 1698, the czar of Russia, Peter the Great, requested Leeuwenhoek to come visit his ship, which was docked nearby, and to bring specimens to view under his remarkable scopes. Leeuwenhoek complied.

Microorganisms on Humans

Another shocking letter Leeuwenhoek wrote to the Royal Society in 1683 avowed that the tiny animalcules that he was now famous for discovering inhabited the human body! Leeuwenhoek prefaced this bold claim by informing his readers of his dental hygiene routine, which included cleaning his teeth daily by rubbing them with salt. Despite this, he still found a whitish sticky substance coating the surfaces of his teeth. When he examined this whitish substance under the microscope, it was teeming with bacteria. When he examined the material from the mouths of people who did not clean their teeth regularly, he found even more creatures, including a new type that resembled a corkscrew. He commented that these creatures might be the cause of bad breath.

This spawned his interest in examining other bodily fluids. He even looked at his own diarrhea (1681) and found what was probably *Giardia*, a flagellated protist that attaches to human intestinal walls with a sucker and causes persistent diarrhea. *Giardia* are *parasitic*, meaning they live off a host, doing harm to the host in the process. However, humans are covered inside and out with many microscopic organisms that cause no harm. These are called *natural flora*, and humans have, in fact, come to depend on many of them. For example, *Escherichia coli* inhabit the intestines. They produce vitamin K and some B vitamins that can be absorbed into the bloodstream and used to benefit the human body. The bacteria benefit from humans as well. They are provided with a safe, warm environment loaded with nutrients. Microorganisms also live in the mouths and on the skin of healthy individuals. While Leeuwenhoek found that microorganisms inhabited many parts of the human body, he never suggested they cause harm. The French scientist Louis Pasteur and the German physician Robert Koch proposed that microorganisms cause disease 200 years later.

Leeuwenhoek also examined semen and was excited to find it loaded with millions of swimming cells, *spermatozoa*. Sperm, for short, are not bacteria or protozoa but are the *gametes* produced by human males. Leeuwenhoek's discovery of these in 1677 shed much light on the then mysterious process of reproduction. He observed sperm in the seminal fluid from a variety of other animals including insects, shellfish, fish, birds, amphibians, and mammals. His studies suggested that sperm cells interact with egg cells from a female to produce offspring. He believed that the female's egg and uterus provided nourishment and shelter for the newly created organism as it grew. This research helped debunk the theory of *spontaneous generation*, which proposed that life arises from nonliving matter.

Though he is most famous for his discovery of microorganisms, Leeuwenhoek also investigated anatomy, reproduction, and nutrient transport in plants. He described the microscopic structure of several types of anatomical structures including what he called air vessels, intestinal tubes, chyle vessels, blood vessels, and nerve tubes. When intrigued by a question of structural anatomy or functional physiology, Leeuwenhoek studied several types of organisms and made comparisons and then generalizations about all living organisms. He studied blood and independently discovered capillaries in 1683. Not being fluent in scientific literature, Leeuwenhoek was unaware of the Italian Marcello Malpighi's discovery in 1661 that capillaries connected arteries with veins. Leeuwenhoek also studied dozens of types of insects and watched spiders spin silk. He studied life cycles of microorganisms, weevils, lice, eels, and other animals.

Precious Scopes Bequeathed

When he was 84 years old, the University of Louvain honored Leeuwenhoek with the presentation of a medal (similar to the giving of an honorary degree) and a tributary poem. He wrote in response that the poem brought tears to his eyes. The father of protozoology and bacteriology died on August 26, 1723, from lung disease, probably pneumonia, and was buried at the Old Church of Delft. On his deathbed, he asked his daughter to deliver the gift of a black cabinet containing 26 finely crafted silver microscopes holding a variety of specimens to the Royal Society. Unfortunately, these microscopes bequeathed to the society vanished, as have most of the hundreds of others Leeuwenhoek so painstakingly crafted. It was 200 years before lenses of magnification and resolution comparable to Leeuwenhoek's were made again.

Today, students learn about Antoni van Leeuwenhoek's discovery of microbial life within the first few chapters of any *microbiology* textbook. Millions have repeated some of his basic examinations, and people continue to be amazed at what they see under the microscope. Since he was never formally educated and had no scientific training, Leeuwenhoek's views were always fresh and unspoiled. Because he understood only Dutch, he was oblivious to the current literature and hardly had any interactions with other scientists outside of his correspondence with the Royal Society, yet he advanced the field of biology greatly due to his natural desire to learn, his finely honed skills, and his ability to describe so vividly and objectively that which he observed.

CHRONOLOGY

1632	Antoni van Leeuwenhoek is born on October 24 in Delft, Holland
1640	Enters school in Warmond
1648	Becomes an apprentice in an Amsterdam cloth shop
1654	Returns to Delft and opens own cloth shop
1660	Becomes chamberlain for the sheriffs of Delft
1669	Becomes a land surveyor for the court of Holland
1671–72	Begins making microscopes
1673	Writes first letter to the Royal Society of London; the correspondence is published in the *Philosophical Transactions of the Royal Society* and begins a 50-year relationship with the Royal Society
1674	Observes "animalcules" for the first time while looking at pond water under a microscope
1677	Discovers sperm cells
1678	Writes to Robert Hooke describing the presence of bacteria in a pepper infusion
1680	Is elected fellow of the Royal Society of London

1698	Peter the Great, the czar of Russia, visits Leeuwenhoek and asks to see a sampling of his remarkable specimens
1699	The Académie des Sciences of Paris nominates Leeuwenhoek a corresponding member
1716	The University of Louvain presents Leeuwenhoek with a medal and a poem
1723	Dies from lung disease on August 26 in Delft

FURTHER READING

Adler, Robert E. *Science Firsts: From the Creation of Science to the Science of Creation.* Hoboken, N.J.: John Wiley & Sons, 2002. Stories of 35 landmark scientific discoveries, including scientific and historical contexts.

De Kruif, Paul. *Microbe Hunters.* San Diego: Harcourt Brace Jovanovich, 1954. A history of the earliest research in bacteriology, revealing the human side of science. Classic text of microbiology written for nonscientists.

Dobell, Clifford. *Antony van Leeuwenhoek and His "Little Animals."* New York: Russell & Russell, 1958. An extensive and accurate account of Leeuwenhoek's life and works. Includes selected translations of his manuscripts and letters.

Ford, Brian J. *Single Lens: The Story of the Simple Microscope.* New York: Harper & Row, 1985. Account written by author who found nine of Leeuwenhoek's original specimen packets and recreated some of Leeuwenhoek's pioneering experiments.

Gillispie, Charles C., ed. *Dictionary of Scientific Biography.* Vol. 8. New York: Scribner, 1970–76. Good source for facts concerning personal backgrounds and scientific accomplishments but assumes reader has basic knowledge of science.

Spangenburg, Ray, and Diane K. Moser. *The History of Science from the Ancient Greeks to the Scientific Revolution.* New York: Facts On File, 2004. Outlines the history of science, building on the ideas of great minds and their predecessors. Intended for middle and high school students.

Waggoner, Ben. "Antony van Leeuwenhoek." Museum of Paleontology, University of California at Berkeley. Available online. URL: http://www.ucmp.berkeley.edu/history/leeuwenhoek.html. Accessed on January 12, 2005. A brief biography containing quotes from some of Leeuwenhoek's letters.

3

Carl Linnaeus
(1707–1778)

Carl Linnaeus is considered the father of taxonomy. (*Library of Congress, Prints and Photographs Division [LC-USZ62-11324]*)

Binomial Nomenclature System

Imagine trying to find one person among a crowd seated in a football stadium, never having seen this person but relying on a physical description from a friend: tall, male, in his late teens, average size build, light brown hair parted on the side, green eyes, a few freckles, roots loudly at athletic events, probably eating a hot dog, and wearing jeans and a navy baseball cap. Locating him based solely on this information would be extremely difficult. If all the people were first arranged into groups according to gender and age, then one might sort them into smaller groups based on hair and eye color or the presence of freckles. The people could be further divided into even smaller groups based on personality traits and preferences such as what they like to wear and eat. Finding the one person would still be quite a task. In the 18th century, a man named Carl Linnaeus volunteered for a similar task. He took it upon himself to create a system for classifying all living organisms. He made it easier for biologists to communicate about such organisms by establishing a means for naming all the organisms and providing very detailed descriptions to distinguish each type of living thing from all others. Even today, the system Linnaeus developed is used as a starting point for classifying and naming newly discovered species.

Little Botanist

On May 23, 1707, Carl Linnaeus was born to a clergyman, Nils Ingemarsson (son of Ingemar) and the daughter of a pastor, Christina, in Råshult, a small town in southern Sweden. In the 18th century, it was common for peasants such as Nils's father not to have surnames. When Nils entered Lund University, he chose the surname Linnaeus, the root of which is "linn," the name of a lime tree in the local dialect. Nils accepted a position as pastor in Stenbrohult, and his family lived in the rectory quarters. Nils was an amateur botanist and kept a beautiful garden. Carl spent time with his father in the garden, playing with flowers. After being admonished by his father for repeatedly asking the names of the same plants, Carl worked hard to remember the names of the plants in his father's gardens and the flowers with which he amused himself in place of toys as a child. Surely this was no easy task, as the names of plants back then were long phrases of Latin words strung together.

Carl had a happy childhood, eventually sharing his home with three little sisters and a little brother. When he was seven, Carl's parents hired a tutor for him, but Carl preferred roaming the meadows near his home rather than studying with his stern teacher. When he was nine, his parents sent him to Växjö, where he remained through high school. He was an average student who obtained the nickname of "little botanist" from his schoolmates. Carl enjoyed natural history and Latin more than the classes that were necessary to prepare for the priesthood, which his parents expected him to enter. In high school, he was introduced to Dr. Johan Rothman, who lectured on logic and physics. Rothman became aware of Carl's interest in *botany*, which was closely linked to medicine, as pharmaceuticals were synthesized from plants. Many physicians had their own gardens from which they treated their patients.

As Carl approached his final year at the high school, his father happened to visit Växjö and speak with Carl's teachers. He was dismayed to learn that they all agreed Carl was not cut out for the priesthood. Downhearted, Nils sought medical attention from Rothman. During his visit, Rothman suggested to him that Carl would make a fine physician, which was not as secure an occupation as being a clergyman, but it gave Nils some hope that his son might still be successful someday. In addition, Rothman offered to take Carl in and mentor him during his last year in Växjö. Rothman offered Carl private lessons in botany and medicine and introduced him to the current system for plant classification proposed by Joseph Pitton de Tournefort. This system was based on the shape of the *corolla*, which is the outer portion of a flower.

The University Years

In 1727, Linnaeus enrolled as a medical student at the University of Lund, his father's alma mater. His impressions of the university were bleak, as there was only one professor of medicine, no botany classes were offered, and the equipment and instruction were lacking. He rented a room at the home of Dr. Kilian Stobaeus, as did another student, David Koulas, who served as Stobaeus's assistant. Stobaeus had a marvelous library, which he kept locked. Koulas sneaked out library books for Linnaeus to read, and in return Linnaeus tutored Koulas in physiology. One night Stobaeus caught Linnaeus reading borrowed library books in his room. He was upset but came to appreciate the budding botanist's desire to learn about the natural world. In approval, he allowed Linnaeus free access to the library and eventually free room and board as well.

Linnaeus went home to Råshult during the summer and was visited by Rothman. When Rothman learned that there were no botany classes at Lund, he encouraged Linnaeus to transfer to the University of Uppsala. The University of Uppsala had a good reputation, but when Linnaeus arrived he found the situation was not much better than Lund. There were two professors of medicine, Lars Roberg and Olaf Rudbeck. Both were old, and Rudbeck did not even lecture anymore but left the teaching of his classes to an assistant, Nils Rosén, who was out of the country obtaining his degree at the time. Linnaeus spent much of his time in the botanical gardens, which were also in a state of ill-repair. One day he was approached by a man who began quizzing him about botany. The man, Dr. Olaf Celsius, dean of the cathedral and professor of theology, was impressed with Linnaeus's answers, and when he learned that Linnaeus had a collection of more than 600 pressed flowers, he invited him to his home. Celsius offered him a room in exchange for his assistance on a book he was writing about biblical plants.

That spring Linnaeus met an older medical student named Peter Artedi. Peter had an excellent academic reputation and enjoyed natural history as much as Linnaeus. The two struck up an extraordinary friendship and spent much time studying together. They even split up the natural world so each could focus their studies on certain subjects and then share their knowledge with each other. Friendly rivalry kept them motivated.

Plant Sexuality

Pupils customarily presented their favorite professors with a poem on New Year's Day. Instead of a simple poem, Linnaeus presented Celsius with a scientific discourse about plant pollination, *Praeludia sponsaliarum plantarum* (Prelude to the betrothal of plants). In it, he explained the roles of plant reproductive structures. *Stamens* are the male parts that consist of a stalk called a *filament* and a terminal sac called the *anther*, which produces the pollen. *Pistils*, also known as carpels, are the female parts of the flower and are made up of the *stigmas*, *styles*, and ovaries. The stigma is located at the tip and is sticky in order to receive pollen. The style is a tubelike structure

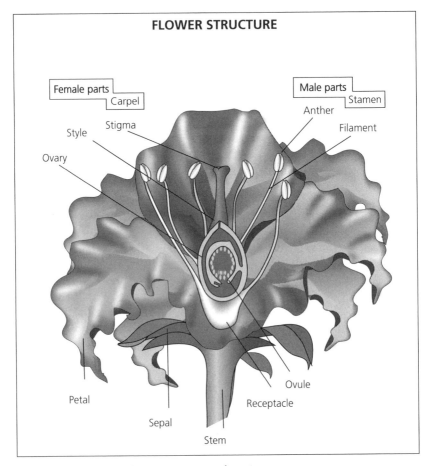

The flower is the reproductive structure of *angiosperms*.

that leads to the *ovary*, which contains the *ovules*, which develop into seeds after fertilization.

In this informal report, he discussed the theory of plant sexuality and compared plant reproduction to animal sex. He compared removing the anthers to castration, the surgical removal of the testicles. He likened pollination by related plants to incestuous relationships and having more than one stamen or pistil to bigamy. While his graphic descriptions offended some, Celsius was so impressed he showed it to Rudbeck, who in turn asked Linnaeus to lecture for him in botany. Though only a second-year student, Linnaeus was in great need of financial assistance and was happy to receive this offer. In addition, Rudbeck hired him to tutor three of his sons (of his total of 24 children from three different marriages).

Linnaeus was quite busy tutoring, lecturing, and tending to his own studies, yet somehow he found time to devote to his love of botany. During his college days, he began composing some of his most renowned works. Linnaeus ordered all the known plants into 24 classes based on the number and position of their stamens. Then he further organized them by the number of pistils they contained and the form of the fruit they bore. For several years, he continued to revise and add to these manuscripts.

In March 1731, Nils Rosén returned to campus, having earned his doctorate in Holland. He expected to take over the botany classes that Linnaeus had been teaching, but Rudbeck let Linnaeus keep them, angering Rosén. Linnaeus was a popular lecturer, which only increased Rosén's jealousy and fueled a decades-long animosity between the two.

Lapland and Europe

The following autumn, Linnaeus was in need of a change of scenery and applied for a small grant to journey to Lapland, an area encompassing the extreme northern portions of Europe, including parts of Sweden, Finland, Norway, and northwest Russia. The Royal Society of Science at Uppsala awarded him money to survey the area for its natural resources. In May 1732, he set off for a four-month-long expedition that was dangerous and uncomfortable. He faced bitter cold, lack of food, and hazardous travel conditions, yet was amazed at the region's enormously rich wildlife. He gathered much information on little-known plants of the region, minerals, and animals as well as Lap customs. He even became a specialist on reindeer habits and discovered more than 100 new plant species. Some of his observations from this influential journey were published in *Flora Lapponica* (Flora of Lapland) in 1737. Others were submitted to the Royal Society but published only in parts. Reports say that the hardships that he claimed to endure on this journey were exaggerated, and at least one of his side trips was completely invented, yet this expedition remains one of the most famous in Sweden.

In 1734, Baron Nils Reuterholm, the chaplain to the provincial governor of Dalarna, invited Linnaeus to survey his province as he had Lapland two years earlier. During a Christmas visit to the home of fellow student Claes Sohlberg, he toured the copper mines in the capital of Falun. Sohlberg's father was the inspector of these mines, which were of interest to Linnaeus since he had taken on lecturing in mineralogy at Uppsala in addition to botany by now. While in Falun, he also met his future wife, Sara Elisabeth, the daughter of Dr. Johan Moraeus. Two weeks after meeting they became engaged, but Moraeus insisted they wait at least three years before marrying.

Sohlberg's father had offered to pay Linnaeus to take his son traveling across Europe and to tutor him. Until this point, Linnaeus apparently saw no reason to speed up the completion of his degree. He was earning just enough money to live, was a respected lecturer at the university, and had written several papers on natural history. Yet he took advantage of this sojourn with Sohlberg through Europe, and in 1735 he ventured off to the Netherlands, where degrees were easily obtained. He had previously written a thesis on the cause of fever, and within two weeks he passed a written and oral examination and received his doctor of medicine degree from the University of Harderwijk.

Organization of Life

Sohlberg and Linnaeus spent three years traveling around Holland, where Linnaeus published numerous botanical papers and met several influential botanists and physicians. Many helped support him, not only financially but also by introducing him to other colleagues and benefactors. In Leiden, he met Jan Frederick Gronovius, who was so impressed with Linnaeus's manuscript *Systema naturae* (System of nature) that he published it for him in 1736. *Systema naturae* presented an outline for classifying the three natural kingdoms: plants, animals, and minerals. The plants were classified according to their sexual systems. For the rest of his life Linnaeus would update and publish new editions of this work. The 12th volume was published in 1768 and included more than 2,300 pages in three volumes. Another popular publication of this time was his *Genera plantarum* (Genera of plants), in which he classified and described all the known plants of the time, approximately 1,000 species. Sohlberg's father never paid Linnaeus, and the two young men drifted apart. Linnaeus found

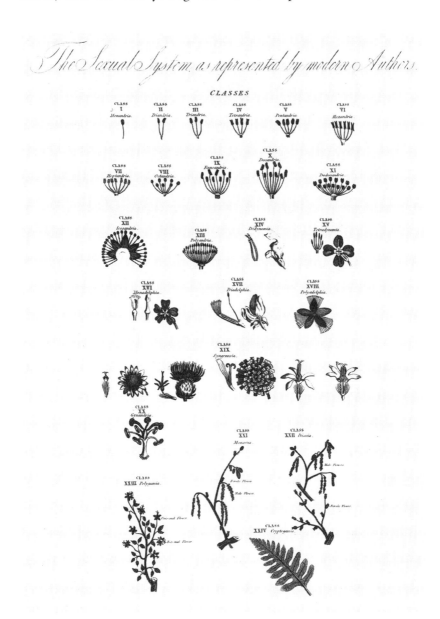

Linnaeus proposed a plant classification system based on reproductive structures. *(Library of Congress, Prints and Photographs Division [LC-USZ62-95191])*

himself dependent upon his growing popularity and his patrons to support himself.

He ventured off to England and soon met a wealthy businessman named George Clifford. Clifford was an enthusiastic botanist as well as the director of the Dutch East India Company. He invited Linnaeus to live with him to oversee his gardens and serve as his personal physician.

While in Holland, Linnaeus by chance encountered his old friend Peter Artedi. Unfortunately, Artedi drowned late one night soon after, and Linnaeus took it upon himself to complete and publish the major effort Artedi was working on at the time, *Ichthyologia*, about the natural history of fishes.

Linnaeus published *Hortus Cliffortianus* (The Clifford garden) in 1737. It contained detailed descriptions of all the plants in Clifford's garden and included illustrations of dissected plants in addition to exacting descriptions of the plants' growth habitats. While this was an extremely tedious and laborious task, Linnaeus was in his element having the opportunity to classify so many plants that he had never seen before.

In the fall of 1737, Linnaeus wanted to return to Sweden, but he became ill and stayed through the winter. After recovering, he eventually made it back to Sara Elisabeth, but only after making several stops in places such as Antwerp, Brussels, and Paris. He also stopped by his home in Stenbrohult, where he proudly showed his father all of his latest publications. Before marrying Sara Elisabeth, he still needed a job.

Physician and Teacher

On the advice of his future father-in-law, Linnaeus set up a medical practice in Stockholm. Potential patients were hesitant to seek medical advice from a young, inexperienced, plant-loving man. One day he happened to talk to a young man whose own physician was unsuccessful in treating his gonorrhea. Linnaeus was able to cure the man within two weeks. Other men soon began to seek his professional advice also, and Linnaeus consulted a French physician for advice on treating sexually transmitted diseases. In addition, he successfully treated a senator's wife for a bad cough. Soon the queen herself was seeking Linnaeus's medical aid. Count Carl Tessin befriended the young doctor and recommended him for the post of physician to the admiralty. A scientific society that was to become the Royal Academy of Sciences was established around this time, and Linnaeus served as the first president. Within a year, Linnaeus was a highly respected physician and had proven he could support Sara Elisabeth. They were married in June 1739, and their first son, Carl, was born in January 1741. They later had three daughters who survived into adulthood.

Professor Roberg eventually retired, and Linnaeus was appointed to replace him. Before moving to Uppsala, however, he went on another expedition to survey the potentially economically profitable natural resources on the Baltic islands of Öland and Gotland. He was hoping to find plants that could be used as dyes and clays that could be used to manufacture porcelain, but he made many other discoveries instead. He learned of a new crop plant, hay seed, how to catch seals, about many local medicinal remedies and farming methods, and how to prevent sand from drifting. He also examined the rock formations, mineral springs, and quicksand.

Afterward, Linnaeus and his family moved to Uppsala, where they would reside for the remainder of their lives. In October 1741, Professor Linnaeus gave his first lecture at the University of Uppsala. Interestingly, it was about the importance of exploring and learning about the natural history of one's homeland. Linnaeus was in charge of botany, dietetics, and *materia medica* (the uses and sources of drugs). He was a very popular lecturer, both publicly and privately. He was captivating, interesting, clear, and even humorous. He encouraged and enjoyed his students, and they enjoyed him.

The botanical gardens on campus had been neglected for many years. There were fewer than 300 cultivated plants at the time. Linnaeus received funding from the senate to repair them as well as build greenhouses and renovate his own home on the garden's grounds. He also enticed Clifford's gardener to come work for him. Over the next decade, the number of specimens in the gardens increased to more than 3,000. Many were gifts from people he had met during his travels and from his students' explorations. Things seemed to go well for Linnaeus, both personally and professionally.

Other faculty members at Uppsala were not too happy with him, however. Perhaps they were jealous of his popularity. They complained about the behavior of his students during his regular Saturday afternoon explorations. In addition, Linnaeus was shunned by some for his explicit sexual comparisons of plants and animals. He did develop one close friendship with a man named Abraham Bäck. They corresponded for many years and visited each other often. Through this correspondence, it was learned that Linnaeus was feeling depressed at this time.

Binomial Nomenclature System

Yet Linnaeus remained prolific. His classic physician's reference on pharmacology, *Materia medica*, was published in 1749. He published more than 170 dissertations on practically every subject of natural history: ants, birds, stones, fossils, crystals, lemmings, grasshoppers, and buckwheat, to name a few. In 1753, *Species plantarum* (Species of plants) was published. This work introduced *binomial nomenclature*, which greatly simplified botanical *taxonomy* and communication among botanists. In binomial nomenclature each species is given a two-word name, the first being the *genus*, the second being the species. These names are given in Latin. The genus is capitalized, while the species name is not. To illustrate this system's utility, consider the following example. Under the old system, one plant was named *Plantago foliis ovato-lanceolatis pubescentibus, spica cylindrical, scapo tereti* (translated "a plantain with pubescent ovate-lanceolate leaves, a cylindric spike, and a terete scape"). Using binomial nomenclature the same plant is referred to simply as *Plantago media*. The generic names are shared among closely related species. The species names distinguish one plant from all other plants in the same genera. Linnaeus often coined names from the surnames of respected colleagues or others he admired. *Species plantarum* included detailed descriptions of the approximately 8,000 known plants at the time, all classified according to his sexual system. His new system was widely adopted over the next few decades.

In Lapland, Linnaeus had observed fishermen searching through hundreds of shellfish to find a single pearl. He noted the potential economic value if one could force their synthesis. He tried to do so by placing a tiny bit of limestone on a wire and inserting it through a small hole into a mussel. He returned the mussel to a riverbed for six years, and when he retrieved it a large beautiful pearl was inside. In 1762, he sold the idea of this process to the Swedish government for a modest price but also for the promise to be able to name his successor at Uppsala. This was his opportunity to secure his son a position. One wonders if he remembers how he had felt when his own parents tried to choose his career, as it is said that the younger Carl was not as interested in botany as he was in women. In any case, the money was enough to pay off a debt he had taken to purchase a summer home, Hammarby. Having lived off the kindness of others for so many years of his younger days, he hated being in debt. In 1761, he was ennobled by the king and took the name Carl von Linné, by which he is remembered in Sweden.

Father of Taxonomy

Shortly thereafter, his health began to fail. Despite this, his wife persuaded him to continue taking on many responsibilities, including rector of the university. He suffered his first angina attack in 1773. In 1774, he suffered his first stroke while giving a lecture and was left partially paralyzed. He began to suffer memory loss, which must have saddened him and his admirers greatly, as he had demonstrated such a tremendous capability for remembering names of obscure plants throughout his entire life.

Linnaeus died following a series of strokes in Uppsala, Sweden, on January 10, 1778. He was buried in the Uppsala cathedral. His family inherited his collections, for which his son cared until his own death six years later. Then his sister sold them to James Smith, an English *naturalist*. Although this infuriated Sweden and Linnaeus's former pupils, Smith had admiration and respect for Linnaeus and founded the Linnean Society of London for the cultivation of the science of natural history. Many of his amazing collections, manuscripts, and correspondence are owned today by the society, and others are housed in various museums across Stockholm, Uppsala, and London.

Biologists consider Linnaeus the father of taxonomy, the science of classification. While his sexual system of classification for plants

Modern Taxonomy

Taxonomy is the field of biology concerned with identifying, classifying, and naming the diversity of life forms. Not only did Linnaeus develop binomial nomenclature, which is still used today, but he established a hierarchical classification system, with each level becoming increasingly more encompassing. Just as organisms evolve, so do methods of naming them. Since the acceptance of the theory of *evolution* by means of *natural selection* that was presented by Charles Darwin in the middle of the 19th century, organisms have been arranged phylogenetically, that is, according to their evolutionary relationships. Scientists originally used detailed studies of *embryology* and comparative anatomy to determine the relationships. Today biologists have much more information by which they formulate classification decisions. For example, molecular methods such as nucleic acid and protein sequencing provide much information regarding evolutionary history.

is no longer used, it brought about many great advances in botany. The method of binomial nomenclature is still used today. The challenges that he undertook were tedious, and his contributions to natural history were enormous. Botanists at the time were anxious to disregard him, and some even ridiculed him, but upon meeting him and observing his unparalleled expertise, they could only respect and admire him. His students revered him, and many eventually became professors themselves.

CHRONOLOGY

| 1707 | Carl Linnaeus is born on May 23 in Råshult, Sweden |
| 1714 | Attends school at Växjö |

The most defined taxonomic group is the species, a group of repro-
ductively isolated groups of organisms. The separation of a species is pre-
dominantly natural, meaning species are principally defined by a
biological mechanism, the ability to reproduce with one another. The
higher levels of classification are man-made. The category above species
is genus. In modern scientific literature, organisms are referred to by their
genus and species as well as a third designation, a letter representing the
person who named the organism. In order of increasing generality, additional levels of classification include families, orders, classes, phyla, kingdoms, and domains. Some of the categories are divided further into
subcategories. For example, human beings belong to the following taxonomic categories: domain of Eukarya, kingdom of Animalia, phylum of
Chordata (subphylum of Vertebrata), class of Mammalia, order of Pri-
mata (suborder of Anthropoidea), family of Hominoidea, genus of
Homo, and species of *sapiens.* In short, humans are referred to scientif-
ically as *Homo sapiens* L. (the "L." stands for Linnaeus, who first named
humans).

1727   Enters the University of Lund

1728   Transfers to the University of Uppsala

1730   Becomes a lecturer in botany at Uppsala

1732   Goes on expedition to Lapland to survey the lands for natural
        resources that might be economically beneficial

1734   Travels to Falun to inspect the copper mines and leads sur-
        veying expedition to Dalarna

1735   Travels to Holland and earns doctor of medicine degree

1736   Publishes *Systema naturae,* which goes through 12 editions in
        his lifetime

1737	Publishes *Flora Lapponica, Genera plantarum,* and *Hortus Cliffortianus*
1738	Returns to Sweden and establishes a medical practice in Stockholm
1739	Becomes the first president of the Royal Swedish Academy of Sciences and is appointed physician to the Admiralty
1741	Goes on expedition to Öland and Gotland
1742	Becomes a professor at the University of Uppsala
1749	Publishes *Materia medica,* a classic pharmacology reference manual for physicians
1753	Publishes *Species plantarum,* introducing binomial nomenclature
1761	Is ennobled and adopts a new name, Carl von Linné
1772	Serves as rector of the University of Uppsala
1778	Dies on January 10 following a series of strokes in Uppsala, Sweden

FURTHER READING

Allaby, Michael, and Derek Gjertsen, eds. *Makers of Science.* Vol. 1. New York: Oxford University Press, 2002. Chronological biographies of influential scientists. Includes political and social settings as well as scientific achievements.

Blunt, Wilfrid. *Linnaeus: The Compleat Naturalist.* Princeton, N.J.: Princeton University Press, 2001. A rounded portrait of the man Linnaeus. Includes 18th-century drawings and illustrations.

Gillispie, Charles C., ed. *Dictionary of Scientific Biography.* Vol. 8. New York: Scribner, 1970–76. Good source for facts concerning personal backgrounds and scientific accomplishments but assumes reader has basic knowledge of science.

Goerke, Heinz. *Linnaeus: A Modern Portrait of the Great Swedish Scientist.* New York: Scribner, 1973. Detailed narrative of Linnaeus's life and his approach to the problems of classification and nomenclature.

The Linnean Society of London homepage. Available online. URL: http://www.linnean.org. Accessed on January 13, 2005. Follow the history link to find a standard brief biography of Linnaeus. Other useful links include one to their current collections.

Olson, Richard, ed. *Biographical Encyclopedia of Scientists*. Vol. 3. New York: Marshall Cavendish, 1998. Contains brief biographies including time lines of significant events.

Scientists and Inventors. New York: Macmillan Library Reference, 1998. Brief profiles of the life and works of more than 100 notable scientists. Written for juvenile readers.

Silverstein, Alvin, and Virginia Silverstein. *Carl Linnaeus: The Man Who Put the World of Life in Order*. New York: John Day, 1969. Biography of the 18th-century Swedish naturalist whose scientific naming of plants and animals provided an international language of nature. Written for young readers.

4

Charles Darwin

(1809–1882)

Charles Darwin proposed the theory of evolution by natural selection. (*Science Photo Library/Photo Researchers, Inc.*)

Natural Selection as a Mechanism for Evolution

The word *evolution* has the power to evoke emotion. Many people mistakenly assume it means the contrary of creation. Evolution simply means change over time, but the focused debate concerning evolution of living organisms, especially of the human species, has given it connotations that oblige people to question their purpose in this world. The theory of evolution forces people to attempt to define the relationship of human beings to the rest of nature. The truth is that living organisms change just as the Earth changes. Charles Darwin formulated the theory of evolution by means of natural selection following a five-year voyage around the world aboard the H.M.S. *Beagle.* When he published his theory in *On the Origin of Species by Means of Natural Selection, or the Preservation of Favoured Races in the Struggle for Life* in 1859, a controversy broke out that lasted until the beginning of the 21st century. While Darwin was not the first to propose that life forms change or evolve, he was the first to propose a scientific mechanism for the process of evolution and to provide an overwhelming amount of organized evidence in support of it.

Divergence from Planned Career

Charles Robert Darwin was born on February 12, 1809, in Shrewsbury, England. His father, Robert, was the son of Erasmus Darwin, a respected physician and nature writer. His mother, Susannah, was the daughter of Josiah Wedgwood, a renowned potter and philanthropist. Both families instilled into their children a high regard for education. This was passed on to Robert and Susannah's own six children, but young Charles was not a promising student.

One year after his mother died, when Charles was nine, his father enrolled him at Shrewsbury School, where his teachers struggled to teach him Latin, the classics, and history. Charles, who preferred to spend his time in a chemistry lab his older brother had fashioned from a tool shed, was terribly bored. Even after the headmaster publicly admonished Charles for wasting his time on scientific pursuits when he should have been studying, Charles did not take a more serious interest in his studies.

When Charles was 16 years old, his father enrolled him at Edinburgh University to study medicine. His older brother was already there, and, after all, his father and grandfather were both successful physicians. Unfortunately, medicine was not to be Charles's destiny. He was disgusted by the animal dissections, and during a mandatory observation of human surgery, he was so repulsed that he ran out of the room. After two years, his father realized that Charles was not going to follow in his footsteps.

Charles next enrolled as a divinity student at Christ's College at Cambridge University. At least this avenue would lead to a respected profession, his father thought. While at Cambridge, Charles continued his personal scientific studies. He also joined the Glutton Club, whose members ate, drank, and played cards frequently. In his spare time he hunted birds and foxes and collected beetles. He successfully completed the requirements for a divinity degree in 1831, but he still needed additional elective credits, so Darwin enrolled in Professor Adam Sedgwick's geology class. For this class he read *A Personal Narrative of Travels to the Equinoctial Regions of the New Continent during the Years 1799–1804* by Alexander von Humboldt. He was fascinated by the voyage of discovery. A botany professor, Reverend John Stevens Henslow, and Sedgwick both recognized Darwin's scientific mind and encouraged Darwin to pursue natural history as a career. However, Darwin could not go against his father's wishes. He earned his bachelor's degree in theology in 1831.

Purpose in a Trip around the World

At the same time, Commander Robert Fitzroy (1805–65) was preparing to depart for South America. Fitzroy was the commander of the H.M.S. *Beagle*, and he was looking for an intellectual companion to spare him from solitary insanity during an upcoming voyage to explore the coasts of South America and the Pacific islands. His friends recommended he bring Darwin along as the voyage's naturalist. Darwin's father initially balked at this idea, but eventually gave in and provided financial support for his son on what would become one of the most influential scientific expeditions of all time.

The H.M.S. *Beagle* set sail from Plymouth, England, on December 27, 1831. Darwin suffered from severe seasickness and spent the first several weeks in the hammock of his cramped cabin. To pass time on board, Darwin read a recently published textbook by Charles Lyell (1797–1875), *The Principles of Geology*. Lyell opposed the popular ideas of the day regarding the history of the Earth. Most scientists believed in the strict biblical account of the creation of the world and the origin of life—God created the world approximately 6,000 years ago, and all organisms were created in their present-day form. Fossils told a different story, one that included the earlier existence of life-forms no longer present. Catastrophists believed that huge earthquakes and floods, such as the one described in Genesis, accounted for the extinction of some species. Lyell did not accept this. He argued that the Earth's current physical form was the result of gradual forces such as erosion and volcanic activity acting over a period of millions of years. Darwin agreed with Lyell. When he voiced his opinions to Fitzroy, Fitzroy was outraged by what he considered blasphemy.

On January 16, 1832, the *Beagle* stopped at the Cape Verde Islands off the northwest coast of Africa. Darwin jumped off board and dutifully performed the tasks he was brought along to accomplish. He wasted no time collecting specimens and taking detailed notes of his observations. Fitzroy was impressed. Darwin also observed evidence in the strata there that supported Lyell's views on the gradual nature of Earth's change.

After a stop at Tenerife of the Canary Islands, the ship arrived in Brazil on February 28, 1832. Darwin was amazed by the wealth of life in the tropical rain forests and struck by the different types of life forms. The crew reached Rio de Janeiro in April, and Darwin noticed the nearby rain forests had been destroyed to accommodate the city's growing population. He was also appalled at the treatment of slaves. He mentioned this to Fitzroy, who vehemently disagreed, causing conflict between the two men. Though Fitzroy later apologized, it was apparent the two men did not have as much in common as they initially thought.

As they traveled down the east coast of South America, Darwin took time to explore the Punta Alta beach, where on September 23, 1832, he discovered the head of a large animal. It took three hours for him to remove it from the rock. The remains turned out to be from an extinct toxodon, a rodent the size of an elephant, similar to the present day capybara, which is about two feet (61 cm) in length. A few days later, he found the bones of a 20-foot-(6-m-) tall ground sloth. Darwin wondered why God bothered to create such similar animals. Why did God destroy the larger ones only to replace them with smaller versions?

Darwin also noticed snakes with tail rattles that were not as efficient as those displayed by the North American rattlesnakes. In

Patagonia, he observed two different forms of unusual ostriches. He also took note of the mountains, valleys, and other geological features of the region. In February of 1835, while in Chile, he experienced an earthquake that destroyed villages and killed inhabitants. The earthquake visibly raised the land level and altered other geological formations. Darwin had witnessed firsthand how an ordinary natural disaster affected the Earth's surface and the life it supported.

On September 15, 1835, the H.M.S. *Beagle* landed at the Galápagos Islands. This isolated equatorial chain of more than a dozen volcanic islands lies 500 miles (800 km) off the west coast of Ecuador. The islands were home to numerous strange animals, animals that were never observed on the mainland of South America and certainly not in Europe. One of the most legendary species inhabiting the Galápagos Islands is the giant tortoise. These tortoises weigh approximately 500 pounds (227 kg) and have shells with a circumference of eight feet (2.4 m). Darwin and his colleagues were easily able to ride on their backs. The tortoises seemed somehow prehistoric to them.

Another famous native of this archipelago is the finch. Darwin observed and sketched 13 different small birds, some of which resembled finches, but others had atypical beaks. He noticed that not only did these birds differ from the mainland birds, but each island seemed to have its own unique species. Darwin found it odd that geologically similar islands would have different species. They all resembled one another, but each variety had a different beak shape. Some were clearly designed for cracking nuts and seed shells. Others were ideally suited for eating insects or fruit. One beak type resembled that of a woodpecker; its shape allowed the bird to extract larvae from tree bark. Darwin again wondered why God would create so many creatures that were very similar yet had discernible differences. He suspected that some natural principle was at work and that God was not the cause.

Late in 1835, the *Beagle* left the Galápagos. They crossed the Pacific Ocean and stopped at Australia. Darwin wondered why kangaroos, wombats, and wallabies lived only in Australia. He had a lifetime's worth of data to examine and many unanswered questions.

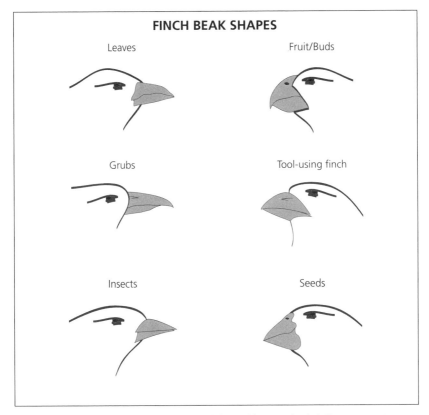

FINCH BEAK SHAPES

Leaves

Fruit/Buds

Grubs

Tool-using finch

Insects

Seeds

Darwin noticed that different islands of the Galápagos had different species of birds, referred to as Darwin's finches, each characterized by a distinct beak shape. Each beak shape was uniquely suited for the diet of that particular species.

Formulation of a Groundbreaking Theory

The ship returned to England on October 2, 1836. Darwin was worried about facing his father. He knew he could not work as a clergyman. His spirit was in science. Upon his return, he was pleasantly surprised to learn that his father was proud of his work as a naturalist. Professor Henslow had been circulating Darwin's correspondence, and he was respected among intellectuals. Darwin was relieved to not have to become a minister and set to work immediately writing up the narrative of his travels. *The Journal of Researches*

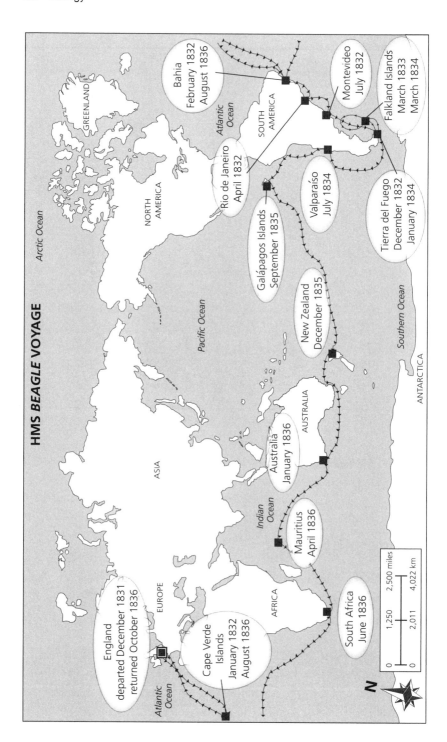

HMS *BEAGLE* VOYAGE

England departed December 1831 returned October 1836

Cape Verde Islands January 1832 August 1836

Bahia February 1832 August 1836

Rio de Janeiro April 1832

Montevideo July 1832

Falkland Islands March 1833 March 1834

Tierra del Fuego December 1832 January 1834

Valparaíso July 1834

Galápagos Islands September 1835

New Zealand December 1835

Australia January 1836

Mauritius April 1836

South Africa June 1836

GREENLAND

NORTH AMERICA

SOUTH AMERICA

EUROPE

AFRICA

ASIA

AUSTRALIA

ANTARCTICA

Arctic Ocean

Atlantic Ocean

Pacific Ocean

Indian Ocean

Southern Ocean

0	1,250	2,500 miles
0	2,011	4,022 km

N

into the Geology and Natural History of the Various Countries Visited by the H.M.S. Beagle *under the Command of Captain Fitzroy, R.N., from 1832–1836* was published in 1839.

Darwin settled back into life in England. He had many observations and specimens that he still needed to process and evaluate. He returned to the question of why so many subtly different forms of animals, such as tortoises, birds, ostriches, and snakes, existed. He concluded that the different forms descended from a single common ancestor. Physical variations slowly accumulated, like geological changes that gradually shaped the Earth. The idea of evolution was not novel. In fact, during the 1770s, Darwin's own grandfather, Erasmus Darwin, had published a book discussing the concept, but the world was not ready to accept evolution. No probable method had been proposed, and there was not enough factual evidence to support the theory. More important, acceptance of evolution required the abandonment of strict biblical teaching. The masses believed that God created the world and all of its species in present form. Darwin knew that in order to convince the world of his theory, he would have to address a persuasive argument posed by those against evolution. The argument stated that organisms were each perfectly suited for the environment in which they lived, and if they did accumulate modifications, these variations would lead them to become less well suited for their habitat. Darwin had to figure out a way that organisms could change so that it looked as if they were designed that way.

Darwin had his work cut out for him. Fortuitously, he had the benefit of several intellectual colleagues with whom he could discuss his ideas. One such colleague was Lyell, whose geology text had influenced Darwin's thinking during the *Beagle* expedition. The two became good friends. Another friend was John Gould, a respected ornithologist. Gould confirmed for Darwin that the Galápagos finches he brought back were all distinct species, not simply slightly different varieties of the same species.

(opposite page) Darwin made observations that led him to develop his theory of evolution by means of natural selection while traveling aboard the H.M.S. *Beagle* on a five-year voyage around the world.

By 1838, Darwin had already spent much time contemplating how offspring differ from their parents. Offspring had subtle yet discernible variations. Darwin thought that if enough of these variations accumulated, it might lead to a new species over thousands of generations. He thought about *artificial selection,* the process in which farmers select domesticated animals or cultivated plants for breeding based on their possession of a desirable characteristic. Over several generations the incidence or degree of the favored characteristic increases. For example, a farmer may choose to breed sheep that yield a superior amount of wool. In the next few generations the sheeps' offspring also would yield more wool.

Darwin also considered extinction. Organisms were thought to become extinct because a change in climate or environmental conditions meant they were no longer perfectly adapted to their environments. Darwin concluded that if some of the offspring had accumulated enough variations, they might have an advantage over those that had not. Then the variant organisms might be better suited to survive in the new environmental conditions. Nature selected against the offspring that were not able to adapt.

In September 1838, Darwin started reading a popular book to give his mind a rest from thinking about evolution. That book was *An Essay on the Principles of Population* by Thomas R. Malthus, an English economist and clergyman. Malthus described how plants and animals produce more offspring than can survive. He discussed human populations and how poverty, famine, and disease acted to keep population size under control. Darwin recognized the significance of the natural struggle for existence.

Animals produce many more offspring than can possibly survive. Those that do survive face a constant struggle for food and territory. Even if they successfully reach adulthood, they then must compete for mates. Offspring that have variations that give them some advantage in their particular environment have a better chance to make it to reproductive age and to breed. Those individuals who are best suited for survival in their environment are the members of that species that pass on their characteristics to the next generation. Since offspring are very similar to their parents, the likelihood is high that they possess the very same characteristics that gave their parents an advantage. In other words, nature selects variations that are advantageous for survival and reproduction in a particular environment, just as farmers artificially select for economically desirable characteristics. Darwin called this process natural selection and believed it was the method by which evolution occurred over thousands of generations. Though this insight would eventually cause a revolution in science, Darwin was hesitant to make it public.

Delay in Publishing New Theory

Darwin had married his cousin, an intelligent woman named Emma Wedgwood, in January 1839. They moved to London and enjoyed an upper-class lifestyle courtesy of wedding gifts from their parents. They eventually had 10 children, only seven of whom survived infancy. Shortly after his wedding, Darwin became mysteriously ill. He was plagued with headaches, fatigue, and sleeplessness. Modern physicians have suggested that he suffered from Chagas disease, a tropical parasitic *infection*, but none of Darwin's doctors could diagnose his illness. The family moved to Down House, Kent, in September 1842, and Darwin retreated from the public.

The year he moved to the Kent countryside, Darwin sketched out his theory of evolution by natural selection in a 35-page outline. In 1844, he expanded it to 230 pages, but he delayed publishing it. Instead, he delved into the study of barnacles for the next eight years. Emma suspected this was a way of avoiding the expected controversy. Darwin knew that though he had collected adequate evidence for evolution and had come up with a plausible method, the masses would reject his theory on religious grounds. Darwin was a shy and now frail man. He did divulge his ideas to a few friends, including Lyell and an English botanist named Joseph Hooker (1817–1911). They encouraged him to continue collecting evidence and developing his theory.

By 1856, Darwin still had not shared his ideas concerning evolution with the rest of the scientific world. Lyell and Hooker exhorted him to publish something before anyone else did. They told him it would be a shame for him to be preempted after two decades of tireless work. So Darwin began slowly writing. Lyell and Hooker urged him to work more rapidly, but Darwin wanted to be thorough.

Then, on June 18, 1858, Darwin received a letter from a young naturalist named Alfred Russel Wallace, who was in the Malay Archipelago at the time. Wallace had developed an idea for how species might change with time, influenced by environmental changes acting to select for advantageous variations in offspring. An essay titled "On the Tendency of Varieties to Depart Indefinitely from the Original Type" was enclosed. Wallace wanted to know if Darwin thought it worthy of publication. Darwin was stunned and shaken! It was as if he were reading a summary of his own book in progress. He appealed to Lyell and Hooker for advice. They acted quickly by presenting both Wallace's essay and Darwin's outline to the Linnean Society on July 17, 1858. Hooker helped to establish priority for his friend by asserting that they had discussed the same ideas more than a dozen years earlier. Surprisingly, Wallace was very chivalrous about this.

Success and Controversy

Now Darwin wrote furiously, producing a 200,000-page manuscript by March 1859. That November, *On the Origin of Species by Means of Natural Selection, or the Preservation of Favoured Races in the Struggle for Life* was published. All 1,250 printed copies sold the first day. The book was very detailed and was composed of three main sections. The first section described the process of natural selection of favorable variations. The second section dealt with objections to common arguments against evolution, such as the lack of transitional forms and the development of complex specialized organs such as eyes. The third section elucidated how the theory of evolution by natural selection explained many previously unexplained phenomena, such as extinction and the slight resemblance of modern and ancient species. *On the Origin of Species* presented immense substantiation for Darwin's theory of evolution by natural selection.

Despite the well-defined supportive arguments and the massive evidence Darwin provided for evolution, his theory engendered a storm of brutal criticism. Famous scientists, including his former professor Sedgwick, English zoologist Richard Owen, and Swiss-American naturalist Louis Agassiz, were all outraged and viciously reviled Darwin and his theory. Darwin had dreaded this outcome

Alfred Russel Wallace

Alfred Russel Wallace, born January 8, 1823, was an English explorer and naturalist who had much in common with Darwin. They had similar childhoods, and like Darwin, Wallace struggled to find a suitable career. Both men earned reputations as naturalists after a scientific voyage. Wallace spent four years on a voyage to South America for the purpose of collecting specimens. Unfortunately, he lost his specimens when his ship caught fire and sank. He achieved success with his published account of the expedition, *A Narrative of Travels on the Amazon and Rio Negro* (1853). Wallace then traveled to the Malay Archipelago, now Indonesia and Malaysia, where he collected more than 125,000 biological specimens. During this trip he wrote to Darwin.

Wallace was struck by the differences between species that lived on the eastern islands and the western islands. He examined their variations and geographical distribution. These observations led him to develop the theory of the origin of species by natural selection, though it was Darwin who coined the phrase. Reading Malthus's essay on human populations also stimulated the development of his ideas, as it did for Darwin. In contrast to Darwin, however, Wallace wasted no time in writing out his ideas. Oblivious to the fact that Darwin was working on the exact same concepts, he sent his essay to Darwin, whom he respected, seeking approval. Both men ended up sharing credit for the theory of evolution by natural selection, but because Darwin had precedence and because he authored the masterpiece *On the Origin of Species by Means of Natural Selection, or the Preservation of Favoured Races in the Struggle for Life,* he is better known.

(continues)

(continued)

Wallace's name was given to the imaginary line that separates the Asian from the Australian and New Guinean fauna. Modern geophysicists have confirmed that this Wallace Line corresponds with the boundaries of tectonic plates. Wallace died on November 7, 1913.

and was predictably upset. Luckily, he found equally aggressive and competent defense from his loyal friends. One such ally was Thomas Henry Huxley (1825–95), a well-known biologist and educator. Huxley was an excellent public speaker and welcomed the challenge of a public debate against Bishop Samuel Wilberforce (1805–73).

The famous debate took place on June 30, 1860, at Oxford University during the annual meeting of the British Association for the Advancement of Science in front of a crowd of more than 700 anxious people. Wilberforce spoke first, denouncing evolution and criticizing Darwin. His speech consisted mostly of personal opinions. The audience applauded loudly and cheered when Wilberforce ended his monologue by asking Huxley if it was through his grandmother or grandfather that he was descended from a monkey.

Huxley spoke next. He pointed out that Wilberforce did not state anything new and did not even appear to understand Darwin's theory or arguments. After carefully reviewing Darwin's theory and clearly presenting the arguments in favor of evolution by natural selection, he ended his speech with the statement that he would rather be descended from an ape than be related to a man bestowed with great intellectual gifts who used them to obscure the truth and mock serious scientific debate. The audience was uncontrollable. Some women fainted. Captain Fitzroy was present. He wildly waved his Bible in the air and yelled abominations against Darwin.

Hooker calmly made his way to the podium. He was disgusted by the behavior of the audience. He proceeded to systematically destroy all of Wilberforce's arguments over a two-hour period. In the end the force of truth prevailed.

ON

THE ORIGIN OF SPECIES

BY MEANS OF NATURAL SELECTION,

OR THE

PRESERVATION OF FAVOURED RACES IN THE STRUGGLE
FOR LIFE.

By CHARLES DARWIN, M.A.,

FELLOW OF THE ROYAL, GEOLOGICAL, LINNÆAN, ETC., SOCIETIES;
AUTHOR OF 'JOURNAL OF RESEARCHES DURING H. M. S. BEAGLE'S VOYAGE
ROUND THE WORLD.'

LONDON:
JOHN MURRAY, ALBEMARLE STREET.
1859.

The right of Translation is reserved.

Darwin's book *On the Origin of Species* sold all of its 1,250 printed copies on
its first day of publication in 1859 and led to a volatile debate that lasted
more than a century. *(Library of Congress, Prints and Photographs Division
[LC-USZ62-95224])*

The controversy continued, however. Darwin left the defense of his ideas up to his qualified contemporaries and spent his time in the gardens of Down House. Though he had deliberately left out any mention of the human species in *On the Origin of Species*, it had become the focus of the debate between creationism and evolution. In 1867, Darwin tackled this directly by composing *The Descent of Man*. This book was published in 1871. Darwin declared that humans and apes had evolved from a common ancestor, but this idea often is represented incorrectly as the idea that man descended from apes. Darwin braced himself for more attacks, but this book did not generate the controversy that *On the Origin of Species* did. Most of the scientific world had already dealt with the notion of human evolution and accepted it as part of evolutionary theory.

The remainder of Darwin's life was deservedly peaceful. He published other works, including *The Expression of the Emotions of Man and Animals* (1872), *Insectivorous Plants* (1875), and *The Movements and Habits of Climbing Plants* (1875). He also wrote an autobiography for his children in 1876 and enjoyed time with his family. His unexplained illness miraculously disappeared. In December 1881, he suffered his first heart seizure. Charles Darwin suffered a second heart seizure and died on April 19, 1882. Though he was elected a member of the Royal Society of London and even awarded their Copley Medal in 1864, he never received formal recognition from the British government while he was alive because his work offended the leaders of the Church of England. Following his death, Parliament requested that he be buried in Westminster Abbey near Sir Isaac Newton.

Today most people have heard of Charles Darwin and consider Darwinism synonymous with evolution. Fundamentalists still decry evolution and fight to suppress its teachings. Amazingly, the negative feelings the general populace harbors concerning evolution are strong enough to force strict guidelines addressing the manner in which it is taught in public schools. However, in the scientific community, evolution by natural selection is a fundamental unifying theory of all the life sciences. Quoting the title of a landmark article written by Theodosius Dobzhansky, a founder of the modern synthesis of evolution, "Nothing in biology makes sense except in the light of evolution."

CHRONOLOGY

1809	Charles Darwin is born on February 10 in Shrewsbury, England
1818	Enters Shrewsbury School
1825–27	Studies medicine at Edinburgh University, Scotland
1828–31	Studies to become a minister at Cambridge University, England
1831–36	*Beagle* voyage around the world
1839	Publishes *The Journal of Researches into the Geology and Natural History of the Various Countries Visited by H.M.S. Beagle under the Command of Captain Fitzroy, R.N., from 1832 to 1836.* The Royal Society of London elects Darwin a fellow
1842	Moves to Down House, Kent, and writes first 35-page draft outlining theory of evolution
1844	Writes 230-page essay outlining his ideas regarding the origin of species
1846–54	Studies barnacles
1858	Receives Alfred Wallace's essay. Papers on evolution by Wallace and Darwin both are read to the Linnean Society. Darwin's priority is established
1859	Publishes *On the Origin of Species by Means of Natural Selection, or the Preservation of Favoured Races in the Struggle for Life.* All 1,250 copies sell the first day
1860	Huxley-Wilberforce debate takes place at Oxford
1871	Publishes *The Descent of Man*
1882	Dies of heart attack on April 10 in Kent and is buried at Westminster Abbey

FURTHER READING

Allaby, Michael, and Derek Gjertsen, eds. *Makers of Science.* Vol 2. New York: Oxford University Press, 2002. Describes the achievements of the world's most famous scientists within their historical contexts. Attractive illustrations.

The Charles Darwin Foundation Homepage. The Charles Darwin Foundation for the Galapagos Islands, 2003. Available online. URL: http://www.darwinfoundation.org. Accessed on January 13, 2005. Very resourceful site. Includes numerous links to articles related to Darwin and current research on the Galápagos Islands.

Darwin, Charles. *On the Origin of Species.* Cambridge, Mass.: Harvard University Press, 1964. Original, classic text that revolutionized science. Highly technical language, written for scientists.

Dobzhansky, Theodosius. "Nothing in Biology Makes Sense Except in the Light of Evolution." *The American Biology Teacher* 35 (1973): 125–29. Easy-to-read essay that emphasizes how evolution unifies the subdisciplines of the biological sciences.

Gillispie, Charles C., ed. *Dictionary of Scientific Biography.* Vol 3. New York: Scribner, 1970–76. Good source for facts concerning personal backgrounds and scientific accomplishments but assumes reader has basic knowledge of science.

Jastrow, Robert. *The Essential Darwin.* Boston: Little, Brown, 1984. Attempts to introduce Darwin's texts to more general audiences, including overviews and explanatory notes.

Nardo, Don. *Charles Darwin.* New York: Chelsea House, 1993. Describes scientific expedition, the development of the theory of evolution by natural selection, and the controversy that followed. Appropriate for young adult readers.

Rice, A. L. *Voyages of Discovery: Three Centuries of Natural History Exploration.* New York: Clarkson Potter, 1999. Visual record chronicling several significant discoveries in natural science exploration. Beautiful artwork and photographs.

5

Gregor Mendel

(1822–1884)

Gregor Mendel is considered the
father of heredity. *(Leslie Holzer/
Photo Researchers, Inc.)*

The Father of Genetics

Everyone has performed experiments in heredity, or, at least, everyone is the product of one. Children receive *genes* from both of their
biological parents. Sometimes the resemblance between family
members is striking; other times it is not. Sometimes a trait that
runs in a family skips a generation and then reappears. People have
wondered how characteristics are transmitted from parents to offspring for thousands of years, and not just in humans, but in domesticated animals and cultivated plants.

An Austrian monk was the first to investigate systematically the transmission of traits and to interpret the results mathematically. Gregor Johann Mendel spent seven years performing cleverly designed pollination experiments on garden peas, resulting in the establishment of the basic laws of heredity. He made his discoveries less than a decade after Charles Darwin published his theory of evolution by means of natural selection. Despite the fact that Mendel's work offered explanations for many unanswered questions concerning Darwin's revolutionary theory, his work went unnoticed for 35 years. When it was rediscovered, it induced a flurry of biological research examining the principles of heredity. Because of this, the modest genius Mendel is considered the father of classical *genetics.*

Son of a Peasant Farmer

Johann Mendel was born on July 22, 1822, in Heinzendorf, which then was part of the Habsburg Empire (now Hynčice, Czech Republic). His father, Anton, had been a soldier in the Austrian army and supported his family as a peasant farmer. His mother, Rosine, was the daughter of a gardener, and she instilled a love for plants in her only son. Johann had an older and a younger sister, and he showed intellectual promise at an early age. In 1833, his schoolmaster recommended he attend the more advanced Piarist secondary school at nearby Leipnik (now Lipnik), 16 miles (26 km) from home. Johann continued to excel, and in 1834 he enrolled at the gymnasium in Troppau (Opava), about 22 miles (35 km) from home.

Johann wanted to become a teacher. After completing six years at the gymnasium, he still needed to complete two years of philosophical studies before he could enroll in a university, but his parents could not afford further schooling. Anton had been injured, and they needed help around the farm. Despite this, Johann chose to support himself and pursue his education rather than become a farmer. His younger sister offered part of her promised dowry so Johann could continue his studies. He also tutored pupils privately to earn money and entered the Philosophical Institute at Olmütz (now Olomouc) in 1841. He was particularly interested in the natural sciences. After two years, he could have enrolled at a university, but he was tired of the constant struggle to make ends meet, so he entered the Augustinian monastery of St. Thomas at Brünn (now Brno), then the capital of the province of Moravia. The recommendation from his professor was so positive that Mendel was admitted without an interview.

Disappointment and Failure

Johann Mendel began his novitiate in October 1843, taking the name Gregor. During the normal probationary period Mendel studied mostly classical subjects, but he pursued his studies of plants and minerals in his free time. He also studied agricultural sciences, as sheep breeding and fruit and wine cultivation formed the basis of the Brno economy. The abbot of the monastery, C. F. Napp, encouraged independent studies and arranged the construction of an experimental garden and a *herbarium* in the monastery.

In 1847, Mendel was ordained a priest. He continued to study theology until 1848, at which time he was made a chaplain of the monastery parish. Mendel, however, was too shy and sensitive to minister effectively to the sick and suffering parishioners. He became physically ill from nerves. Napp took pity on him and appointed him to teach the classics and mathematics to seventh graders in the town of Znojmo (Znaim) in southern Moravia. Mendel was excited to have this opportunity. He wanted to teach natural history. He performed very well and gladly accepted a position as a substitute teacher at the Znojmo Gymnasium in 1849. He was a patient teacher and impressed the faculty with his efforts. In order to be appointed a regular teacher, however, Mendel had to pass a competence exam.

Obtaining a teaching certificate turned out to be Mendel's albatross. He did well on his physics and meteorology exams but failed the *zoology* and geology portions. Two explanations for his failure were that he did not have the advantage of a university education and that he had attempted to prepare on his own while teaching a full load of courses. Despite this letdown, he had a good reputation as a teacher. The following year he substituted for an ill natural history teacher at the Brno Technical School. During his time in Brno, Mendel became an extraordinary member for the Natural Science Section of the Agricultural Society.

When Mendel was 29 years old, Napp sent him to Vienna University to prepare further for his teacher's qualifying examination. During the period 1851–53, Mendel mostly studied physics but also took mathematics, chemistry, zoology, botany, plant physiology, and paleontology. He was particularly interested in botany and plant hybridization, but his studies in physics and mathematics also greatly influenced his later work. In physics he discovered the simplicity of natural laws, and in mathematics he learned to use probability theory and statistical analysis.

After completing his studies at Vienna, he returned to the monastery in July 1853. It is not known why he did not retake his teacher's qualifying exam immediately. A post opened up at the Realschule, a nontraditional technical school, and he taught physics and natural history there for the next 14 years. Mendel also took charge of the natural science collections. His expertise with specialized flora was admired, and he often took students on botanical excursions. Mendel did attempt to retake the qualifying exam in 1855, but he failed a second time, most likely due to nerves. He continued teaching, but without a full appointment, he earned only half-pay.

Revelation of the Secrets of Heredity

It is hard to imagine that Mendel had any free time, but he managed to initiate a series of independent studies at the monastery. In the early 1850s, he started performing artificial pollinations with *Pisum*, the ordinary garden pea, to determine how traits were passed from generation to generation. In 1854, he became a full member of the Natural Science Section of the Agricultural Society in Brno, which later evolved into the Natural Science Society. The economic aspects of plant hybridization thrust the topic into the spotlight at the society's meetings. Mendel began a series of experiments for which the purpose was to examine the transfer of traits between generations. The results of these experiments led to the formulation of the laws of heredity, which form the basis of the field of genetics. Mendel presented his findings during two lectures for the Natural Science Society in February and March 1865.

With great care Mendel selected *Pisum* to use in his breeding experiments. The plants were simple to grow, he could easily control pollinations, they had several easily distinguishable characteristics to examine, and the *hybrids* were fertile. Hybrids are new varieties of plants created by crossing two distinct varieties or species. Mendel spent two years ensuring that the 34 varieties of peas he planned to use were true-breeding, meaning self-pollination resulted in the constancy of specific traits generation after generation. The seven characteristics chosen for analysis were seed shape, seed color, flower color, pod shape, pod color, flower position, and stem length. Mendel also made sure to collect huge amounts of data to eliminate any misleading effects due to chance. Over a seven-year period, he cultivated and studied almost 30,000 plants.

Starting with a single pair of traits, Mendel began his methodical pollinations. First, he pollinated round-seeded pea plants with pollen from wrinkled-seeded plants. All the seeds produced were round. When he performed the *reciprocal cross*, that is, when he pollinated plants of wrinkled-seeded peas with pollen from round-seeded plants, the same results were observed. (The hybrid offspring from these initial crosses are often referred to as the F_1 generation.) Next, Mendel planted the round hybrid seeds and allowed them to self-fertilize. (The offspring of the hybrid are often referred to as the F_2 generation.) The self-fertilizations resulted in 5,474 round and 1,850 wrinkled seeds. Though the wrinkled seeds had seemed to vanish in the previous generation, now they reappeared. Mendel called the trait that prevailed after the first set of crosses "dominating" (now called *dominant*), and the trait that disappeared for a generation he called *recessive.*

Mendel performed similar experiments to examine the transmittance of the other six traits and obtained similar results. In all cases, one of the traits was dominant and the other recessive. More remarkably, all hybrid F_2 offspring exhibited a 3:1 ratio of the dominant to the recessive trait. These findings were important because at the time many scientists believed that inherited characteristics were an intermediate form of expression of the parental traits. This data clearly showed that the parents' traits were not blended in the hybrids.

MENDEL'S RESULTS

Trait	Dominant quantity	Recessive quantity	Total	Ratio Dominant : Recessive
Seed shape	5,474	1,850	7,324	2.96 : 1
Seed color	6,022	2,001	8,023	3.01 : 1
Seed coat color	705	224	929	3.15 : 1
Pod shape	882	299	1,181	2.95 : 1
Pod color	428	152	580	2.82 : 1
Flower position	651	207	858	3.14 : 1
Stem length	787	277	1,064	2.84 : 1

Mendel observed a 3:1 segregation ratio in the hybrid progeny for all seven traits he examined.

Mendel did not stop there; he let the F_2 plants self-fertilize. Keeping very meticulous records, he examined all the offspring of the resultant F_3 generation. In the data, he recognized that the 3:1 ratio of observed characteristics, or *phenotypes*, was really a disguised 1:2:1 ratio. He concluded that each trait in an individual resulted from the combination of a pair of discrete units (today called *alleles*). Each parent contributed one unit for each trait to the offspring. These were transmitted to the offspring by the gametes, the sex cells that fuse during fertilization. Because each parent possessed two alleles for each particular trait, there was a 50 percent chance that the offspring would inherit either specific allele from that parent.

Mendel devised a method of alphabetical notation that is still used today. Each unit, or allele, was represented by a letter. For example, he used "*A*" for the trait of round or wrinkled seeds. The uppercase "*A*" signified the dominant allele, in this case, the allele that encoded the round phenotype. The lowercase form of the letter, "*a*," symbolized the recessive form of the trait. Thus, each individual organism contained a pair of alleles that together determined whether the seeds would be round or wrinkled. There are three possible *genotypes*, or combinations of alleles, that an individual might possess: *AA*, *Aa*, or *aa*. The two combinations that have two of the same alleles (*AA* and *aa*) are called *homozygous* genotypes, whereas the combination of the two different alleles (*Aa*) is termed *heterozygous*. The heterozygous genotype leads to the dominant phenotype. In other words, plants with the *Aa* genotype will have round seeds.

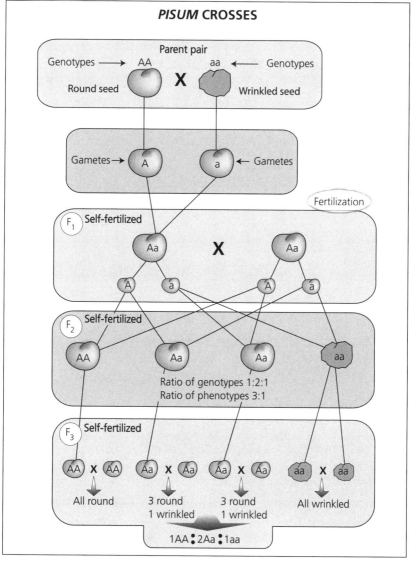

PISUM CROSSES

Mendel used true-breeding parents to obtain hybrid F₁ offspring and then allowed the F₁ to self-fertilize in order to obtain the F₂ generation. Further controlled self-fertilizations revealed the parental genotypes.

Using this notation and terminology, it is easier to describe what happened in Mendel's pea crosses. He started with *true-breeding* plants, meaning the genotypes were homozygous. When he crossed the true-breeding parents with each other ($AA \times aa$), all the offspring inherited one dominant and one recessive allele. Thus, all the hybrid offspring in the F_1 generation were heterozygous, Aa, and had the round phenotype.

In the second set of crosses, Mendel used the heterozygous F_1s as the parents ($Aa \times Aa$). Since these individuals possessed both alleles, they were capable of contributing either the dominant or the recessive allele to their offspring. This led to three possible genotypes in the F_2 generation: AA, Aa, or aa. Both the AA and Aa genotypes encoded the round phenotype, but the combination of

Too Good to Be True?

Beginning around 1911, Mendel's data began to stir up controversy. Throughout the 1900s, there were several attempts to show that his data were not realistic. The data were too good to be true! Critics suggested that Mendel either failed to report some of his data or fabricated his numbers. His data fit the expected ratios better than chance alone predicted. Numerical analysis rarely would yield results so close to the expected values. For example, if someone flips a coin 200 times, what are the chances that 100 of those events will reveal heads and 100 will reveal tails? Using principles of probability, one could calculate the likelihood of getting exactly 100 heads and 100 tails on 200 coin tosses to be approximately 5.63 percent. Perhaps the coin would land on heads 95 times and tails 105 times, or 111 and 89. Though the expectation of achieving a 3:1 ratio in Mendel's pea crosses has been proven correct over time by a preponderance of evidence, statistical analysis reveals that the probability that the actual outcome would be so close to the expected is quite low. A

two recessive alleles allowed the recessive phenotype of wrinkled seeds to reappear after skipping one generation. The phenotypic ratio of offspring in the F_2 was 3 round:1 wrinkled. Mendel had the remarkable insight to recognize a 1 *AA*:2 *Aa*:1 *aa* genotypic ratio hidden within this 3:1 phenotypic ratio.

To verify the genotypes, Mendel performed backcrosses of the hybrids with the recessive true-breeding parent. A backcross is a cross of an individual with one of its parents or another organism with the same genotype as one of its parents. Since the recessive true-breeding parent could contribute only the recessive allele to its offspring, the appearance of any offspring with the recessive phenotype necessitated a heterozygous parent. He also performed reciprocal crosses, meaning the genotype of the female in the first

detailed statistical analysis performed by British scientist Ronald Fisher purported that the probability that Mendel would have achieved his published results by chance alone was only 1 in 30,000.

Some scientists believed that Mendel adjusted his data to fit his hypothesis. They thought his numbers were too close to the predicted 3:1 ratio. Perhaps Mendel subconsciously sorted plants with questionable phenotypes into the category that favored his hypothesis. Maybe an assistant did so. At any rate, Mendel was an experienced teacher and probably left out what he considered extraneous information from his landmark paper. He did not feel obligated to report all the details and deleted those that did not contribute to his main points. Everything known about Mendel personally indicates he did not manipulate the numbers dishonestly. Whether or not he presented skewed results to emphasize his point, Mendel is to be admired for his brilliant insight. No other scientists had performed such meticulous experiments and predicted or explained the outcome. No one else before him or for 35 years afterward had perceived the 3:1 ratio as a 1:2:1 ratio. No one else deserves the credit for transforming a seemingly random set of phenomena into a logical set of laws of heredity.

cross was presented as the genotype of the male parent in the second cross. It did not matter which phenotype (or genotype) was used to pollinate, the results were always the same. From this series of experiments, the law of *segregation* was formulated. The law of segregation states that the allele pairs separate during gamete formation and then randomly re-form pairs during the fusion of gametes at fertilization.

The brilliant scientist next wondered what the result would be if he examined two traits at the same time. He started by crossing plants that bred true for both seed shape and color. Round and yellow (*AABB*) were crossed with wrinkled and green (*aabb*). As expected, considering that the F_1 genotypes must have been *AaBb*, all the offspring exhibited the dominant phenotypes of being round and yellow. These offspring, which were heterozygous for both traits, were allowed to self-fertilize. This sort of cross is called a dihybrid cross. When Mendel performed this experiment, he obtained four different phenotypes in the F_2 generation that occurred in the ratio of 9 round and yellow:3 round and green:3 wrinkled and yellow:1 wrinkled and green. When looked at separately, the two traits still exhibited a 3:1 phenotypic ratio.

In order to gain information concerning the genotypes of the F_2 generation, he allowed them to self-fertilize. From this experiment he determined that there were nine different genotypes in the F_2 occurring in the ratio of 1 *AABB*:2 *AABb*:1 *AAbb*:2 *AaBB*:4 *AaBb*:2 *Aabb*:1 *aaBB*:2 *aaBb*:1 *aabb*. Each trait independently exhibited the same behavior as when monohybrid crosses were performed. The transmittance of the alleles for one trait had no effect on the transmittance of the alleles for a second trait. He performed similar experiments pairing all of the different traits with one another. Each time the traits segregated into a 9:3:3:1 phenotypic ratio and a 1:2:1:2:4:2:1:2:1 genotypic ratio in the F_2. From these observations, Mendel formulated what is now known as the law of *independent assortment*. The law of independent assortment states that each allele pair segregates independently during gamete formation. Today we know this law applies only when the two traits being examined are located on different chromosomes or are sufficiently distant from each other on the same chromosome.

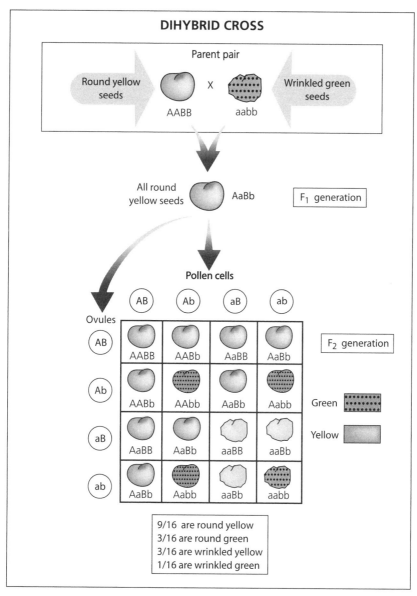

DIHYBRID CROSS

Parent pair

Round yellow seeds X Wrinkled green seeds

AABB   aabb

All round yellow seeds AaBb   F₁ generation

Pollen cells

AB Ab aB ab

Ovules

AB   AABB AABb AaBB AaBb   F₂ generation

Ab   AABb AAbb AaBb Aabb   Green

aB   AaBB AaBb aaBB aaBb   Yellow

ab   AaBb Aabb aaBb aabb

9/16 are round yellow
3/16 are round green
3/16 are wrinkled yellow
1/16 are wrinkled green

The 9:3:3:1 phenotypic ratio of a dihybrid cross demonstrated that alleles for one gene segregated independently of alleles for other genes.

The lectures Mendel presented in 1865 were published the following year in the Natural Science Society's *Proceedings*. Neither the lectures nor his paper aroused much interest. Because this was a rather obscure journal, the paper went largely unnoticed following its publication. In addition, neither the members of the society nor the rest of the world were intellectually prepared for the mathematical methodology or far-reaching implications of Mendel's research. It is known that evolutionary theorist Charles Darwin received a copy of the paper, but he probably never read it.

The powerful deductions contained in the paper "Experiments with Plant Hybrids" are summarized as follows.

- Hereditary determinants are individually distinct in nature. Today these determinants are known as genes.
- Genes exist in pairs. Each adult plant carries two copies, or alleles, of each gene for a specific trait.
- The alleles may be two types, dominant or recessive. An individual can have two alleles of the same type or one copy of each.
- The members of a gene pair separate equally during gamete formation. Consequently, each gamete carries only one member of a gene pair.
- The union of gametes is random.

These concepts form the basic principles of genetics. They are the simplest guidelines, to which many exceptions have since been discovered.

Meteorology and Bees

Though he is most famous for his experiments in plant breeding, Mendel also was considered an authority on meteorology. He was a member of the Vienna Meteorological Society and took daily observations at the monastery. Beginning in 1857, he meticulously recorded data including temperature, rainfall, air pressure, and ozone levels, but he also noted wind direction as indicated by a flag posted on a nearby tower and wind force as determined by the smoke coming from chimneys across the horizon. He generated a tabular overview of this data, which he presented to the Natural Science Society in 1862. This graphical summary was quite popular among other amateur meteorologists. Mendel also enjoyed using statistical analysis to forecast the weather for farmers. A paper from

1870 that described the causes of tornadoes demonstrated his scientific approach to meteorology.

In 1863, Mendel became a member of the Brno Agricultural Society. In 1868, he was elected abbot of the monastery to replace Napp, who had passed away. Without teaching anymore, he thought he would have more time to devote to his research, but the duties of his new position were very consuming. His views on many political matters conflicted with the government's opinions, and he was not a very popular public figure. He joined the Society of Apiculturists in 1870 and studied heredity in bees. He hoped to find that the principles he developed while studying plants also applied to animals. This endeavor was unsuccessful due to the complex mating behavior of bees.

Though he never married, family was important to Mendel. He enjoyed playing chess with his nephews and regularly corresponded with all his family members. He repaid the debt to his younger sister, who shared her dowry to support his education, by financing the college educations of her three sons. Mendel's health declined near the end of 1883. His kidneys and his heart failed. On January 6, 1884, Mendel died without ever having received recognition for his remarkable insight into the laws of heredity. His remains were interred in the monastery tomb in the Central Cemetery.

Thirty-Five Years Later

Mendel made one of the most significant discoveries in biology in 1865, and 35 years later its historical significance was finally brought to light. At the turn of the century, three separate researchers were independently researching similar phenomena when they stumbled upon Mendel's paper. The Dutch botanist Hugo de Vries, the German botanist Carl Correns, and the Austrian botanist Erich von Tschermak all thought they had attained novel results when they read Mendel's findings. The English biologist William Bateson also deserves some credit for exposing Mendel's original research. In 1902, he published *Mendel's Principles of Heredity, a Defense* and coined the term *genetics*, defined as the study of the mechanisms of inheritance. Though all of these men recognized the significance of Mendel's work, whereas his 19th-century counterparts did not, none of them had devised the idea of pairs of discrete units to represent each trait.

Following his rediscovery, a statue of Mendel was erected outside the monastery in Brno in 1910. In 1922, a sandstone monument was placed in Mendel's experimental garden. To celebrate the centennial, Brno hosted a Mendel Memorial Symposium in 1965. The Mendelianum, part of the Moravian Museum in Brno, opened. In 2002, a new international exhibition, the Mendel Museum of Genetics, was established in the Abbey of St. Thomas in Brno, where Mendel lived and worked. There the world can visit to pay their respects to the unrecognized, humble genius and his discoveries.

CHRONOLOGY

1822	Johann Mendel is born on July 22 in Heinzendorf, Silesia, part of the Habsburg Empire
1840	Graduates from the gymnasium in Troppau
1841	Enrolls at Philosophical Institute in Olmütz
1843	Enters the Augustinian monastery of St. Thomas in Brünn, taking the name Gregor
1847	Is ordained a priest
1849	Starts teaching Greek and mathematics at a school in Znojmo
1850	Fails the exam for teacher's certification
1851–53	Studies natural history at the University of Vienna
1854	Becomes a member of the Natural Science Section of the Agricultural Society, which later becomes the Natural Science Society
1854–68	Teaches natural history and physics at Realschule
1855	Fails the teacher's qualifying exam a second time
1856	Begins breeding experiments with peas
1865	Presents his experimental results on *Pisum* crosses to the Natural Science Society on February 8 and March 8

1866	Publishes his results, "Experiments with Plant Hybrids," in the society's *Proceedings*
1868	Replaces C. F. Napp as abbot of the monastery
1884	Dies on January 6 at Brünn
1900	Mendel's work is rediscovered, and its significance is finally recognized

FURTHER READING

Aaseng, Nathan. *Genetics: Unlocking the Secrets of Life.* Minneapolis, Minn.: Oliver Press, 1996. Traces the development of the field of genetics. Includes chapters summarizing contributions of scientists including Darwin, Mendel, Morgan, Avery, Watson and Crick, and Khorana.

Allaby, Michael, and Derek Gjertsen, eds. *Makers of Science.* Vol. 2. New York: Oxford University Press, 2002. Describes the achievements of the world's most famous scientists within their historical contexts. Attractive illustrations.

Blumberg, Roger B. Mendelweb Homepage. Available online. URL: http://www.mendelweb.org. Accessed on January 13, 2005. Wonderful educational resource for anyone interested in the origins of classical genetics, introductory data analysis, elementary plant science, and the history and literature of science. Contains links to a translation of Mendel's original paper, "Experiments in Plant Hybridization," and links to several commentaries about his research.

Edelson, Edward. *Gregor Mendel and the Roots of Genetics.* New York: Oxford University Press, 1999. Describes Mendel's life and how the field of genetics was built upon his discoveries. Written for middle and high school students.

Henig, Robin Marantz. *The Monk in the Garden: The Lost and Found Genius of Gregor Mendel, the Father of Genetics.* Boston: Houghton Mifflin, 2000. Mendel's discovery recounted in the form of a suspenseful narrative.

Orel, Vítězslav. *Gregor Mendel: The First Geneticist.* Oxford: Oxford University Press, 1996. Account of Mendel's life and work with attention to the social, political, and intellectual environment. Not clearly presented, but authoritative.

Saari, Peggy, and Stephen Allison, eds. *The Lives and Works of 150 Scientists*. Vol. 2. Detroit: U*X*L, 1996. Alphabetically arranged introductions to the contributions of scientists from a variety of fields. Intended for middle school students.

Thomas Hunt Morgan

6

(1866–1945)

Thomas Hunt Morgan provided overwhelming experimental evidence in support of Mendelian theory and the chromosome theory of inheritance. (© *The Nobel Foundation*)

The Roles of Genes and Chromosomes in Heredity

Though people have wondered about breeding and inheritance for centuries, the field of genetics has been around for only 150 years. Geneticists research everything from inherited disorders to evolutionary relationships among species, from chromosomal structure to molecules that turn genes on or off. The science of genetics consists of many subfields including classical genetics, molecular genetics, population genetics, and evolutionary genetics.

Thomas Hunt Morgan headed a research team that essentially created the subfield of classical genetics. He is responsible for providing overwhelming evidence in support of Mendelian theory and the chromosome theory. His research on fruit flies firmly established the basic laws of inheritance. He also proved that genes were physical entities that existed on chromosomes in a linear arrangement with measurable distances between them and discovered *sex-linked* inheritance. For his numerous advances in the field of genetics, Morgan was awarded the Nobel Prize in physiology or medicine in 1933.

A Famous Family

Thomas Hunt Morgan was born on September 25, 1866, in Lexington, Kentucky. He was the oldest son of Charlton Hunt Morgan and Ellen Key Howard. His family was well known, as his uncle was a famous Confederate Army general and his great-grandfather was Francis Scott Key, composer of "The Star-Spangled Banner." The Morgans later had two more children. As a child Tom enjoyed the outdoors and especially collecting natural treasures such as fossils and butterflies near a relative's summer home in Oakland, Maryland.

During his teenage years Tom spent two summers working for the U.S. Geological Survey in the Kentucky mountains. After two preparatory years at the State College of Kentucky, he began course work toward a bachelor of science degree in zoology. The members of the all-male student body were military cadets. The routine and expectations were strict, and Tom received his share of demerits. The science program was limited, but Tom excelled. He earned his degree summa cum laude in 1886 and was voted valedictorian for his graduating class of three total members.

Before starting graduate school Morgan spent the summer studying marine biology at the Boston Society of Natural History's marine biological station in Annisquam, Massachusetts. This station was the precursor to the Marine Biological Laboratory at Woods Hole. There he developed an interest in marine life that persisted throughout his scientific career. He entered Johns Hopkins University that fall. Though only a decade old, Johns Hopkins had an excellent academic reputation and was one of very few American colleges that concentrated on biology as a science. The faculty emphasized the importance of inquiry and laboratory research. Biology was in the process of transforming from a descriptive discipline to an experimental science.

Sea Spiders and Frog Eggs

As a doctoral candidate, Morgan studied embryology, the study of embryos, or animals during early development. The goal of his research was to classify sea spiders, *Pycnogonida*. A morphological, or structural, approach suggested they were crustaceans, a class that includes aquatic animals such as crabs, lobsters, and crayfish. Morgan took a comparative embryological approach. By comparing their anatomies during different stages of development, he determined that sea spiders more closely resembled arachnids, a class including true spiders and scorpions.

After completing two years of graduate study at Johns Hopkins, Morgan was eligible for a master of science degree from the State College of Kentucky. The only requirements were two years of study at another institution and a satisfactory examination by the college faculty. The faculty was so impressed with Morgan that they offered him an immediate position as a professor. They were presumptuous enough to list him in the catalog as a professor of natural history! However, Morgan chose to pursue his schooling.

He earned a Ph.D. in 1890 for work on the development and classification of sea spiders and was awarded a one-year postdoctoral research fellowship. He spent the following year conducting research and traveling to the Bahamas, Jamaica, and the zoological station in Naples, Italy. Morgan's training from Johns Hopkins taught him to be mentally flexible, to accept as true only that which had been thoroughly examined, and to reject that which was false. Science left no room for subjectivity or emotional attachments to merely fashionable theories.

In 1891, Morgan took a position as an associate professor of biology at Bryn Mawr College, an intellectually rigorous college for women in Pennsylvania. As a teacher he was well liked, but he was not a very organized lecturer. He lectured as if he were thinking aloud. The students either loved or hated his classes, and he always welcomed those seeking extra help.

Embryological studies of marine animals remained the focus of his research at Bryn Mawr. He studied sea acorns, frogs, and ascidian worms. His research convinced him that biology needed to advance to more experimental analysis rather than remain simply descriptive. Morgan examined the processes by which sea urchin eggs duplicated and differentiated into multicellular, multifunctional adults. He found that developmental cues were mostly intrinsic to the organism. Gravity did not play an important role in the early development, as some scientists thought. The role of most environmental influences was comparatively small.

In 1894, Morgan returned to Naples for a year. After this sabbatical he was promoted to full professor. He published his first book in 1897, *The Development of the Frog's Egg: An Introduction to Experimental Embryology*. That same year he was elected to the board of trustees for the Marine Biological Laboratory at Woods Hole, which was rapidly becoming a mecca for marine biological research. He remained an active board member until 1937. In 1901, Morgan published *Regeneration*, a book that summarized the current state of knowledge on the subject of regeneration, the process by which body parts are replaced by new tissue growth. For example, if a sea star loses one of its arms due to injury, it will grow another one in its place. Morgan likened the process of regeneration to embryological development and emphasized the importance of experimental analysis in discovering natural laws that governed both processes. He also published *Evolution and Adaptation* in 1903. In this book, Morgan attacked the theory of evolution by means of natural selection as proposed by English naturalist Charles Darwin, claiming there were too many loopholes. Later in life, he came to accept the theory and even published others books on the topic, tying together the concepts of heredity and evolution by natural selection: *A Critique of the Theory of Evolution* (1916) and *The Scientific Basis of Evolution* (1932).

When he was offered a position as chair of experimental zoology at Columbia University in New York in 1904, Morgan accepted it. Before moving, he married an 1891 Bryn Mawr alumna named Lilian Vaughan Sampson. They eventually had four children together. After the children were all in school, Lilian earned a fine reputation as a cell biologist.

At Columbia Morgan continued to study sea urchins in order to examine the question of whether environment or heredity played a larger role in embryonic development. His research showed inheritance was more important, sparking his interest in heredity. Another hot research topic at the time was the mechanism of sex determination. Some scientists believed that environment controlled the outcome of an organism's sex, while others believed it was heredity. Morgan followed this scientific debate with interest.

The Dawn of Genetics

Heredity was an exciting new field of research. The work of Austrian monk Gregor Mendel had been rediscovered in 1900. Mendel had proposed that specific factors (today called genes) were responsible for inherited characteristics. He said that individuals had two copies of each gene and that the members of each gene pair separated during gamete (sex cell) production so that offspring received one member from each parent. The members of the gene pair, or alleles, could be dominant or recessive. Dominant characteristics were expressed even if only one dominant allele were inherited, while recessive alleles were outwardly expressed only if both inherited alleles were recessive. Morgan did not immediately accept Mendelian theory. Typical of his personality, he required very definite experimental evidence to accept anything, more evidence than had been provided to date. Ironically, Morgan would be the one to provide the overwhelming evidence in support of Mendel's theory.

One of Mendel's rediscoverers, the German botanist Carl Correns, hypothesized that chromosomes, prominent structures located within the nucleus of cells, might contain genes. In 1903, the American cytologist Walter Sutton published a paper firmly stating that the behavior of chromosomes during the cellular process of *meiosis* exemplified the behavior of Mendel's factors of inheritance. (Meiosis is the process of making gametes, or eggs and sperm cells.) The following year, the German biologist Theodor Boveri corroborated these conclusions. Most of the world immediately accepted that

Sex Determination Mechanisms

Whether an organism turns out to be male or female is the result of a complicated series of precisely controlled developmental processes. In some species environmental mechanisms play a major role in the determination of sex. For example, the incubation temperature of turtle eggs during a critical phase in embryogenesis determines the sex of the hatchling. Generally, cooler nest temperatures result in a higher number of males, whereas warmer nests produce more females. Oyster sex can switch in response to changes in environmental factors such as food supply or water temperature. Slipper limpets, a type of gastropod sea mollusk, form stacks that attach to seashore rocks. The sex of individual slipper limpets is determined by their relative position in the stack.

The sex of other organisms is determined chromosomally. There are four methods of chromosomal sex determination: XY, ZW, XO, and compound chromosomal mechanisms. The alphabetical notation is completely symbolic. The letters signify nothing about the size or shape of the chromosomes they represent. Humans and fruit flies follow the XY sys-

genes were located on chromosomes, ushering in the era of the chromosome theory of inheritance. However, Morgan remained cautious.

A cytogeneticist working at Bryn Mawr named Nettie Maria Stevens hypothesized that the sex of an organism was determined by the inheritance of a specific sex chromosome. The sex chromosomes are termed the "X" and the "Y" chromosomes. She performed experiments to confirm her hypothesis using the yellow meal worm beetle, *Tenebrio molitor*, as a model organism. She determined that sperm carried either an X or a Y chromosome, while eggs all carried X chromosomes, and she showed that when an egg was fertilized by a sperm carrying the Y chromosome, a male organ-

tem. In this system, females are the *homomorphic* sex, meaning they have two X chromosomes (XX), and males are *heteromorphic,* meaning they have one X and one Y chromosome (XY).

More precisely, in fruit flies, the genic balance, or the ratio of the number of X chromosomes to autosomal (nonsex) pairs of chromosomes (X:A), determines the sex outcome. The work leading to the genic balance theory was mostly performed by an undergraduate student, Calvin B. Bridges, in Morgan's laboratory. Normally, if the X:A ratio is 1.0 or higher, then the outcome will be female. If the ratio is 0.5 or lower, the organism will be male. If the ratio is between 0.5 and 1.0, the organism is considered intersex.

In the ZW system the males are homomorphic (ZZ), and females are heteromorphic (ZW). Birds and moths follow the ZW mechanism. Animals such as some grasshoppers, which follow the XO mechanism, have only one type of one sex chromosome. Usually females have two copies, and males have only one. Lastly, some species of beetles and bedbugs carry several X and Y chromosomes that collectively determine the sex. This is the compound chromosomal method of sex determination. While the genes carried by the sex chromosomes initiate the process of sexual development, many other genetic and hormonal influences ultimately affect the outcome.

ism resulted. When an egg was fertilized by a sperm carrying an X chromosome, a female resulted. She then expanded her studies to include different species. Working independently, a colleague and friend of Morgan at Columbia, Edmund Beecher Wilson, also demonstrated that the sex of an organism was determined chromosomally using the seed bug *Lygaeus furcicus* as a model organism.

In the Eye of a Fly

Morgan started using fruit flies, *Drosophila,* as a model system around 1908. These flies were optimal research material since their

Drosophila melanogaster is commonly used in genetic research because it is small in size and easy to breed in large numbers. *(Dr. Jeremy Burgess/Science Photo Library/Photo Researchers, Inc.)*

generation time was only two weeks long, they were easy to breed, they were cheap to maintain in the lab, they did not require much laboratory space, and they had only four pairs of chromosomes. One of Morgan's graduate students, Fernandus Payne, was trying to produce blind mutants by culturing flies in the dark. After breeding 69 generations in the dark without success, the student tried inducing mutations by exposing them to X-rays, radium, and various environmental conditions with no luck. Then in 1910 something noteworthy occurred.

In May 1910, a white-eyed male fly was born in Morgan's laboratory. The source of this fly has been disputed, but Morgan certainly knew what to do with it. He mated this male fly with a normal red-eyed female. All 1,240 of the offspring had red eyes. (Actually, three did have white eyes but are believed to have been the result of spontaneous mutation.) In Mendelian terms, this meant that the red-eyed phenotype (observed characteristic) was dominant to white eyes. Next, he mated the red-eyed offspring (F_1) with one another and found the white-eyed phenotype reappeared in the next generation (F_2). According to Mendel's research, the recessive phenotype was expected to reappear in one-fourth of the offspring. This was what Morgan observed, but interestingly, though one-fourth of all the offspring had white eyes, all of them were males. None of the female flies had white eyes. Though in the past he had argued against Mendel's conclusions, Morgan's work actually

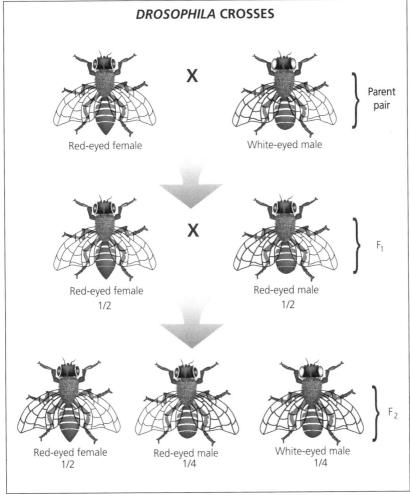

DROSOPHILA CROSSES

X

Red-eyed female

White-eyed male

} Parent pair

X

Red-eyed female
1/2

Red-eyed male
1/2

} F_1

Red-eyed female
1/2

Red-eyed male
1/4

White-eyed male
1/4

} F_2

Breeding experiments using a white-eyed mutant male showed that eye color was a sex-linked trait in *Drosophila*.

provided overwhelming evidence in support of Mendel's laws and the chromosomal theory of inheritance.

Morgan correctly concluded that the gene controlling eye color was located on the X chromosome. Today, genes located on either the X or Y sex chromosomes are referred to as sex-linked. Since male flies possessed only one X chromosome, a recessive allele for white eyes would not be masked. Females have two X chromosomes and thus are likely to have a dominant red-eyed allele that would prevent the outward expression of the recessive white-eyed phenotype. The females in the F_1 generation must have possessed one X chromosome containing a dominant allele and one X chromosome with a recessive allele. Today, organisms that possess both a recessive allele and a dominant allele and have the dominant phenotype are called *carriers*. These experiments clearly demonstrated that specific genes are associated with specific chromosomes and that certain genes are sex-linked. This work also contributed to our understanding of genetic sex determining mechanisms.

Gene Mapping

Following the success of these experiments, the members of Morgan's laboratory excitedly performed more breeding experiments with *Drosophila*. Two undergraduate students, Alfred H. Sturtevant and Calvin B. Bridges, and a graduate student named Hermann Joseph Muller performed the bulk of the labor. They spent winters at Columbia and summers at Woods Hole. The two labs were affectionately referred to as the "fly room." Together Morgan's team began finding a few new mutations each month. By 1912, they had discovered 40 types of flies with mutations such as crooked or tiny wings and yellow bodies.

Each new mutant type was mated methodically, and the progeny were mated with their siblings, their parents, and with other mutants. It soon became apparent that these mutations were inherited in groups. Since the fruit fly has four different chromosomes, there were four groups, each corresponding to a particular chromosome. All the mutants were carefully classed. The data supported the hypothesis that traits were linked with other traits. Furthermore, the number of genes in a linkage group correlated with the length of the associated chromosome. Morgan imagined the genes were arranged in a linear fashion along the length of a chromosome, like beads on a string.

As their research progressed, the team began to notice that traits thought to be linked, that is, grouped together on the same chromosome, sometimes were inherited independently. Furthermore, some genes appeared more tightly linked than others. How could this be? An astute observer, Morgan also noticed that chromosomes occasionally appeared visibly tangled during the process of meiosis. In 1909, the Belgian cytologist F. A. Janssens had described this intertwining of chromosomes during meiosis and claimed that parts of the chromosomes physically exchanged fragments during the process. Morgan called this event crossing over, or *recombination*.

Sturtevant brilliantly related the frequency of these events to the distance between genes. Genes that were distant to one another along the length of a chromosome had a greater chance of becoming "unlinked" during meiosis than did genes that were near to one another. In other words, the greater the distance between two genes, the more space in which a break could occur. Morgan's lab members performed numerous crosses of flies with mutations of linked genes, calculated the frequency of the linked traits segregating, and from this estimated the genetic distance between the genes. The unit for such chromosome mapping measurements is called the centimorgan, in Morgan's honor. The mapping work clearly demonstrated that genes exist in a linear arrangement on chromosomes.

Exceptions to Mendelian theory arose that complicated interpretation of the fly room's data. Lethal genes caused the embryos to die before birth. Some genes were found to have multiple alleles, not simply one dominant and the other recessive. Other traits were affected by more than one gene. The concept of crossover interference was proposed to explain why some crossover frequencies did not turn out as expected based on genetic distances. All of these situations have been studied thoroughly and now are accepted as common modifications to Mendelian inheritance. Sturtevant suspected that the position of a gene on a chromosome affected its expression. This suggestion was furiously refuted by staunch Mendel supporters, though it later proved to be a real effect.

In addition to his numerous peer-reviewed papers in renowned scientific journals, Morgan published several textbooks that shaped the field of genetics. A joint effort of Morgan, Bridges, Sturtevant, and Muller, *Mechanism of Mendelian Heredity*, was published in 1915. This book was Morgan's best-known work. It clearly described the relationship between genes and chromosomes and outlined the role of chromosomes in heredity. It also helped to establish genetics as an experimental rather than descriptive science. In 1926, Morgan published *The Theory of the Gene*, which clearly summarized all that had been discovered regarding the transmission of traits to offspring. Though Morgan was very proud of a text he wrote in 1927, *Experimental Embryology*, it was not as popular as his books about genetics. The world considered Morgan a geneticist, whereas he thought of himself more broadly as an experimental zoologist.

In 1927, the California Institute of Technology invited Morgan to Pasadena to found a new division of biology. He could not refuse this opportunity to establish an entire department based on his own philosophies about biology and the importance of experimental analysis. Much of his lab followed him, and he remained there for the rest of his career. His research after moving to California focused on embryological issues, such as egg cleavage and factors that affect development. He began his scientific career as an embryologist and ended his research career studying embryology.

First Geneticist to Receive a Nobel Prize

Morgan was awarded the Nobel Prize in physiology or medicine in 1933 for his advances in genetics. He generously shared the prize money with his former students and lifelong coworkers, Bridges and Sturtevant, to support their children's college education. Though his genetic discoveries that led to the Nobel Prize are his most famous, it is important to remember that Morgan made significant contributions to the fields of embryology and developmental biology as well. He was a remarkable, multitalented scientist who was respected and admired by his colleagues. Because of this he was elected a member of numerous scientific organizations and served as president for several, including the prestigious National Academy of Sciences (1927–28) and the Association for the Advancement of Sciences (1929). He was awarded both the Darwin Medal (1924) and the Copley Medal (1939) from the Royal Society of London.

Though he officially retired from Cal Tech in 1942, Morgan continued with his administrative responsibilities until his death in 1945. His cause of death was a ruptured artery following a severe attack from a chronic ulcer. His body was cremated, and the family held a small private memorial service.

Because of Thomas Hunt Morgan's research, geneticists have a better understanding of the physical entity of the gene and how genes are transmitted from generation to generation. Genetic counselors can educate affected families about the probability of having offspring with sex-linked disorders such as hemophilia and color blindness. The mapping of genes for other genetic disorders is possible due to Morgan's extraordinary progress.

Morgan and his students performed a remarkable number of experiments that lent unquestionable support to Mendel's laws of inheritance and generated huge amounts of data that greatly advanced the science of genetics. Surprisingly, however, his name is not as generally known as are other pioneers in biology, such as Gregor Mendel and Charles Darwin. Perhaps this is because Morgan's personal life was rather normal. His individual quirks were limited to belting his pants with rope and leaving his hair disheveled. He was stingy with institutional and governmental funds, but he was generous with his own wealth. Thankfully, he was also generous with his scientific talents.

CHRONOLOGY

1866   Thomas Hunt Morgan is born on September 25 in Lexington, Kentucky

1886   Obtains a bachelor of science degree in zoology from the State College of Kentucky (now the University of Kentucky) and spends the summer at the Boston Society of Natural History's marine biological station at Annisquam, Massachusetts

1888	Earns a master of science degree from State College of Kentucky in absentia
1890	Receives a Ph.D. for research on the evolutionary relationships of sea spiders from Johns Hopkins University
1891– 1904	Studies embryological development and regeneration as an associate professor of biology at Bryn Mawr College
1897	Publishes first book, *The Development of the Frog's Egg: An Introduction to Experimental Embryology*
1903	Publishes *Evolution and Adaptation,* attacking the theory of natural selection
1904–28	Serves as chair and professor of experimental zoology at Columbia University in New York
1910	Begins research on heredity in fruit flies, which leads to his publishing numerous landmark articles on *Drosophila* genetics
1915	Publishes a fundamental genetics textbook, *The Mechanism of Mendelian Heredity,* with Bridges, Sturtevant, and Muller, defining the roles of genes and chromosomes in heredity
1916	Publishes *Sex-linked Inheritance in* Drosophila and *A Critique of the Theory of Evolution,* which genetically explains natural selection in terms of mutations
1925	Publishes *Evolution and Genetics* and *The Genetics of Drosophila,* sometimes considered the bible of geneticists
1926	Summarizes the entire field of genetics, including his own numerous contributions, in the book *The Theory of the Gene*
1928	Sets up a new division of biological sciences at the California Institute of Technology, serving as director until his death
1933	Receives the Nobel Prize in physiology or medicine for his discoveries concerning the role played by chromosomes in heredity
1945	Dies on December 4 at Pasadena, California

FURTHER READING

Aaseng, Nathan. *Genetics: Unlocking the Secrets of Life.* Minneapolis, Minn.: Oliver Press, 1996. Traces the development of the field of genetics. Includes chapters summarizing contributions of scientists including Darwin, Mendel, Morgan, Avery, Watson and Crick, and Khorana.

Allen, Garland E. *Thomas Hunt Morgan: The Man and His Science.* Princeton, N.J.: Princeton University Press, 1978. Complete portrayal of Morgan's personal and professional life. Difficult reading.

Ellavich, Marie C., ed. *Scientists: Their Lives and Works.* Vol. 6. Detroit: U*X*L, 1999. Introductions to the contributions of scientists from a variety of fields. Intended for middle and high school students.

Gillispie, Charles C., ed. *Dictionary of Scientific Biography.* Vol. 9. New York: Scribner, 1970–76. Good source for facts concerning personal backgrounds and scientific accomplishments but assumes reader has basic knowledge of science.

Nobelprize.org. "The Nobel Prize in Physiology or Medicine 1933." Available online. URL: http://www.nobelprize.org/medicine/laureates/1933. Last modified on June 16, 2000. Includes biography, banquet speech, article, and other references.

Shine, Ian, and Sylvia Wrobel. *Thomas Hunt Morgan: Pioneer of Genetics.* Lexington: University Press of Kentucky, 1976. Description of Morgan's most noted works and his approach toward science with a useful summary of accomplishments and personality in the conclusion.

7
Charles Henry Turner
(1867–1923)

Charles Henry Turner was an entomologist who demonstrated that insects can hear and learn. *(Graciously provided from the collection at the Saint Louis Science Center)*

Insect Behavior

Behavior describes how organisms respond to environmental stimuli such as chemicals, light, sounds, smells, touch, or the actions of other organisms. In animals, behaviors may be inborn (instinctive) or learned, but most are a combination of both. For tens of thousands of years, in order to improve their capture of *prey* and to avoid becoming prey, humans have observed the behavior of animals, but the scientific study of animal behavior, *ethology*, originated only after the turn of the 20th century. An *entomologist* (a scientist who studies insects) named Charles Henry Turner was a devoted researcher who overcame obstacles, including lack of funding and equipment and racial discrimination, to perform pioneering research in the field of animal behavior. He studied a wide variety of bugs, including ants, bees, cockroaches, moths, and spiders and discovered that insects can hear, see colors, and learn by trial and error.

A Janitor's Son

Charles Henry Turner was born on February 3, 1867, in Cincinnati, Ohio. His father, Thomas Turner, was a church janitor from Canada who amassed an impressive literary collection that he shared with his son. His mother, Adeline (Addie) Campbell Turner, was a nurse who had been born in the slave state of Kentucky. The Civil War had ended just two years prior to Charles's birth.

After graduating as valedictorian of his high school, Turner enrolled at the University of Cincinnati, where he struggled academically during his first year. He eventually came under the tutelage of the biology professor and pioneering psychobiologist Clarence Luther Herrick. Herrick was impressed by Turner and published his undergraduate thesis, "Morphology of the Avian Brain," in the first issue of *Journal of Comparative Neurology* in 1891. Turner also studied gallery spiders, today called funnel weavers because they weave funnels in their webs in which they hide while waiting for prey. He observed that the spiders built webs of different shapes depending on the environmental conditions rather than simply out of *instinct*. For example, Turner repeatedly knocked down a web that one spider kept building by a windowsill. After being destroyed four times, the spider built the fifth web in a more discrete location underneath the windowsill. Turner also observed different custom-built shapes in a variety of hunting-ground locations and concluded that spiders were more intelligent than had been previously assumed.

While he was still an undergraduate, he took a short leave of absence (1888–89) and taught fifth grade at the Governor Street School in Evansville, Indiana, and also substituted in the Cincinnati public grammar schools. Turner earned a bachelor's degree in biology in 1891 and a master's in zoology the following year from the University of Cincinnati. After graduating he worked as an assistant instructor in the biology laboratory (1891–93).

In 1887, Turner married Leontine Troy. They had three children together before she died following a period of mental illness in 1895. He then married Lillian Porter of Augusta, Georgia, in 1907 or 1908. She survived Turner and died in 1946.

After obtaining his master's degree, Turner was hired as a biology professor at Clark University (today called Clark Atlanta University) in Atlanta, Georgia. He taught at Clark from 1893 until 1905 and then took a job as principal of College Hill High School in Cleveland, Tennessee, for one year. From 1907 to 1908 he taught biology and chemistry at the Haines Normal and Industrial Institute in Augusta, and in 1908 he moved to St. Louis, Missouri, where he taught biology and psychology for the remainder of his career at the all-black Sumner High School and Teacher's College. He believed that he would be more valuable teaching other African Americans than in a profession where he could devote more time to scientific research. He used progressive teaching methods, often bringing in live animal and plant specimens for direct observation, and encouraged his students to explore them using microscopes. On evenings and during vacations from school, Turner performed research on insect behavior. His experiments were many and varied in content, but they were always distinguished and valuable.

Homing in Ants

While teaching, Turner pursued his doctoral degree. He went to the University of Chicago in 1898 but returned to Clark the following year, planning to continue his graduate studies in absentia. In 1907, Turner received his doctorate in zoology from the University of Chicago, one of the first African Americans to earn a doctorate in the biological sciences. His notable dissertation, "The Homing of Ants: An Experimental Study in Ant Behavior," was published in the *Journal of Comparative Neurology and Psychology*. This analysis, which he presented at the International Zoological Conference in Boston, was his first significant independent research study and marked the turning point in his research from classical studies on structure and function to animal behavior.

Ants have the ability to find their way back home after traveling some distance in search of food. Turner wondered how they were able to do so. Was it instinct? Was it by scent, landmark recognition, or sunlight? While observing ants crawling on a vine on a brick wall near his home, he ripped off a leaf that had an ant on it and stuck it in a hole two feet away from its original location. The ant crawled all over the place in a seemingly random fashion until it finally found its home. After several repeated attempts, Turner found no evidence that ants were able to find their way home by instinct.

In order to see if smell played a significant role in guiding ants home, he set up a cardboard platform with an inclined bridge leading to a nest. He placed ants and immature young on the platform, knowing the adult ants would try to get them back to the safety of the nest as quickly as possible, and allowed them time to learn the pathway to get to the nest. After they did so, he added another inclined bridge leading from the opposite side of the platform to the nest, but none of the ants used the new route. To see if the ants left a scent trail that guided other ants, he then switched the ramps, so the one the ants had been using (that might contain an odor) was in the position of the ramp that no ants had used and the unused ramp was on the side of the platform that the ants had been using. The ants continued to use the incline placed in the same pathway as they had been taking previously, indicating that scent was not a major factor in pathfinding.

To test directly whether light played a role in homing or pathfinding, Turner designed an experiment in which a nest was placed near two lighted ramps. The light bulbs were heat-filtered to ensure that temperature would not interfere with the interpretation of results. He placed *pupae*, larvae, eggs, and some ants on a platform between the ramps. Turner alternated which ramp was lighted and kept track of which ramp the ants used to carry the larvae and eggs back to their nest. Though they appeared slightly confused initially after Turner switched which ramp was lighted, the ants always traveled the lighted ramp, in more than 100 trials. This experiment showed that light was one factor for ants in choosing a route to the

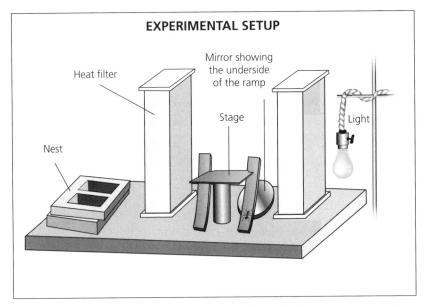

EXPERIMENTAL SETUP

Heat filter

Mirror showing the underside of the ramp

Stage

Light

Nest

Turner used a raised platform with ramps on either side to examine the mechanism by which ants found their nests.

nest. He also tested ramps with different textures and odors and concluded that light, touch, and smells other than from ants themselves all played a role.

Tropisms are involuntary movements that occur in living organisms in response to external stimuli, such as light or touch. Turner demonstrated that some invertebrates demonstrated a circling movement when excited. He described a unique gyrating pattern performed by ants; they circled as they returned to their nest. Because Turner was the first to describe this characteristic action, French zoologists named it *Turner's circling*.

Bee Behavior

Several of Turner's honey bee experiments are his most famous. A former pupil described one experiment in which Turner set dishes of jam on a picnic table three times a day, and bees visited all three times. After a while, he stopped setting out the jam at lunch time and dinner time. Bees initially continued to appear at those times but then only came at breakfast time, demonstrating that bees can learn and also have a sense of time.

A particular species of bee burrows in ground nests, and Turner wondered how they found their nest. According to one of his pupils, on the way to school Turner observed a bee entering a hole in the ground, then reappearing and flying away, presumably to collect more pollen for storage. While the bee was gone, Turner used a stick to make a second hole in the ground and then placed a bottle cap that had been next to the original hole near the new hole. When the bee returned, it entered the new hole, the one with the bottle cap nearby. It immediately came back out, appearing confused, and then found its original hole. After it left again, Turner made several more holes and proceeded to place the bottle cap in different positions. The bee had trouble finding the correct hole and had to fly in and out of each one randomly to locate the correct one.

To explore further the means by which bees recognized their ground nests, Turner next arranged a piece of white paper with a hole in the center so the hole was directly over the bee's nest entrance. When a bee appeared, it hesitated and hovered for a few minutes before entering the hole. As it was preparing to depart again, Turner noted that the bee hovered over the entrance for a bit, as if taking a memory picture of the opening. When the bee returned, it entered the nest without hesitation, as if it remembered the hole's surroundings. Turner then used a piece of watermelon rind with a circular region cut out and a tented piece of white paper situated over the hole. In all instances when Turner varied the features surrounding the nest entrance, the bee seemed to take memory pictures in order to recognize the area. Changes to the topography (topography is the physical form surrounding a region) surrounding the hole appeared to confuse the bee.

Biologists knew that bees were attracted to particular types of flowers by their scent. Turner wanted to learn whether sight also played a role. Previous experiments designed to determine whether bees could recognize colors gave ambiguous and sometimes contradictory results. To determine whether bees could distinguish colors, Turner attached red circular discs to wooden sticks to simulate flowers. He dripped some honey on each one, and after a few hours bees began to visit the makeshift flowers and lap up the honey from them. Then Turner set out blue discs among the red ones, but he did not dribble them with honey. Bees ignored them. When he did put some honey on a blue disc, it took a while before the bees fed from it. Turner suspected they had learned that red meant honey-bearing whereas blue meant not-honey-bearing and that color vision played a role in drawing bees from a distance, whereas odor may be more significant when nearby. After demonstrating that bees had color vision, he extended his studies by using different geometric patterns instead of different colors and showed that bees could recognize patterns as well. He concluded that bees may be attracted by flower color and shape in addition to scent.

Tricky Trappers

The pit-making ant lion reportedly was Turner's favorite insect. An ant lion, or doodlebug, is a plump, hairy insect larva that has pro-truding jaws and can only walk backward. Ant lions exhibit an inter-esting behavior in which they back into a mound of sand while using their tails as shovels to push sand aside and a back-and-forth head motion to displace the sand further. In this manner, they exca-vate a pit. The insect hides in the bottom of the pit, and if an ant crawls over the pitted area the weakened sand gives way and the vic-tim plunges into the pit, where the ant lion kills it and sucks out its body juices for nourishment.

While observing this behavior, Turner witnessed the ant lions striking a death pose, a motionless posture that others might mis-take for death. After much careful observation, he concluded that the insects were not actually playing dead but rather were tem-porarily paralyzed out of terror. Turner became known as an expert on ant lions.

Learning in Cockroaches and Moths

In order to determine if cockroaches had the ability to learn, Turner designed a flat metal maze with four blind alleys. When he placed a cockroach at one end, it proceeded to select random routes until it found the jelly jar that it considered home. A bath of water was placed under the maze, so if the roaches departed from the maze they landed in the water. Turner counted the mistakes, meaning turns into blind alleys or drops into the water, and wiped the maze with rubbing alcohol to remove any scent trail between trials. The first few attempts resulted in several falls into the water. A roach initially took between 15 and 60 minutes to complete the maze, but after many runs it could complete the maze in one to four minutes. Turner concluded that if a roach completed the maze three times in a row without any mistakes, it had learned the route. Within one day a roach could learn the pathway through the maze to the jar, proving roaches could learn by trial and error. He also discovered that if they were kept off the maze for 12 hours, the roaches forgot the path.

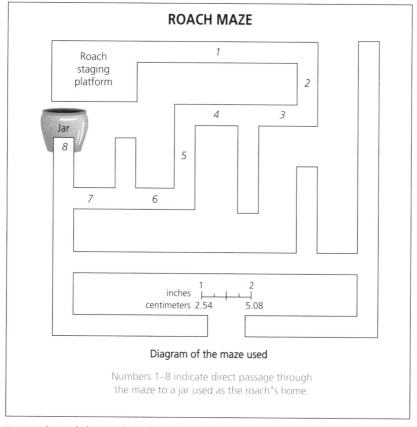

ROACH MAZE

Diagram of the maze used

Numbers 1–8 indicate direct passage through the maze to a jar used as the roach's home.

Turner showed that cockroaches were capable of learning the pathway through a maze that was suspended over water.

Cockroaches are nocturnal animals, meaning they are most active at night, and they naturally avoid light. Turner attempted to train the insects to avoid dark instead. He did this by setting up a device that administered an electric shock to the roaches when they entered a dark area. Over time they learned to avoid the dark.

Turner also was successful teaching moths to relate low-pitched sounds from an organ pipe to a food reward, demonstrating not only that moths could learn from experience, but also that they could distinguish pitch. (He used a whistle to create higher-pitched sounds.)

Animal Behavior Pioneers

The field of animal behavior was not recognized as a unique subfield of the biological sciences until the middle of the 20th century, when three pioneers started studying behavior by scientific methodology, using systematic observation and experimentation. Lorenz, von Frisch, and Tinbergen shared the Nobel Prize in physiology or medicine in 1973 for their discoveries concerning organization and elicitation of individual and social behavior patterns.

Austrian naturalist Konrad Lorenz (1903–89) helped found the field of animal behavior by studying geese. Lorenz described *imprinting,* a behavior in which young animals learn to identify and then bond with their parent within a short period of time. When the parents are removed within a few days of birth, the goslings recognize any moving object as their mother. Lorenz raised goslings that bonded with him and followed him around as if he were their parent.

German scientist Karl von Frisch (1886–1982) studied communication in honeybees for 60 years. He found that bees are genetically

A Dedicated Researcher

Charles Henry Turner died on February 14, 1923, in Chicago, Illinois. Though he never held a faculty position at a primarily academic research institution, he conducted quality independent research for his entire career. He worked without assistance, financial support, or fancy equipment, yet he published more than 50 research articles and several reviews on the behavior of insects and other invertebrate animals. He was the first African American elected to the St. Louis Academy of Sciences and was an honorary member of the Illinois Academy of Science and the Entomological Society of America.

programmed to perform waggle dances that communicate to other bees in their hive that food is near, as well as signaling the direction and the distance of nectar-bearing flowers. To indicate direction, the bees use ultraviolet rays emitted from the sun that are not visible to the human eye.

Nikolaas Tinbergen (1907–88) of the United Kingdom performed famous field experiments that explored the mechanism by which digger wasps found their nests. Knowing that female wasps visit their nests daily to bring food to their larvae, he set up a ring of pinecones around the entrance to a ground nest. After the wasp departed the nest, he moved the circle of pinecones a few feet over. When the female wasp returned, she immediately flew to the center of the ring of pinecones instead of to the nest's actual entrance that was just a few feet away. In another experiment, after the wasp departed the nest he arranged the pinecones into a triangle around the nest entrance rather than a circle and set up a circle of stones a few feet away. When the wasp returned, it flew to the center of the circle of stones rather than the triangle of pinecones that actually surrounded the nest. These experiments suggested that wasps find their nests by recognizing the arrangement of visual landmarks near the hole.

Though Turner was dedicated to his scientific research, he also was active in black organizations and served as director of the Colored Branch of the St. Louis YMCA. He strongly believed that education was of paramount importance in the advancement of African Americans within the community and wrote articles on the subject. At the time of his death, Turner was composing a novel. He had also found time to write a children's book on nature studies and a book of poems.

Turner's groundbreaking research into the behavior of insects was emulated by many. Unfortunately, because he was ahead of his time in the not-yet-recognized field of animal behavior, many ethologists who followed were unaware of Turner's findings that insects could learn, his descriptions of honeybee feeding habits, and his observations on homing in ants. Though he may not have received due recognition for his scientific research, as a highly educated black man who spoke out for civil rights he inspired many. In Turner's honor, a school in St. Louis for physically disabled children was named for him in 1925, the Charles Henry Turner Open Air School for Crippled Children. In 1954, it became the Turner Middle Branch School. In 1999, the Charles Henry Turner MEGA (Multimedia Electronic Graphic Arts) Magnet Middle School was founded.

CHRONOLOGY

1867 Charles Henry Turner is born on February 3 in Cincinnati, Ohio

1886 Enrolls at the University of Cincinnati

1888–89 Takes a leave of absence and teaches fifth grade at the Governor Street School in Evansville, Indiana

1891 Earns bachelor of science degree in biology from the University of Cincinnati. Publishes his undergraduate thesis, a paper titled "Morphology of the Avian Brain," in the inaugural issue of *Journal of Comparative Neurology*

1891–93 Works as an assistant instructor in the biology laboratory at the University of Cincinnati

1892   Publishes "Psychological Notes upon the Gallery Spider" in *The Journal of Comparative Neurology* and earns master's degree in zoology from the University of Cincinnati

1893   Becomes a professor of biology and chair of science at Clark University (now Clark Atlanta University) in Georgia

1905–06 Accepts position as the principal at College Hill High School in Cleveland, Tennessee

1907   Earns his doctorate in zoology from the University of Chicago and serves as a delegate to the Seventh International Zoological Congress in Boston and as secretary to the animal behavior section

1907–08 Works as a professor of biology and chemistry at the Haines Normal and Industrial Institute in Augusta, Georgia

1908–22 Teaches high school at Sumner High School in St. Louis, Missouri

1910   Publishes "Experiments on Color-Vision of the Honey Bee" in *Biological Bulletin,* showing that bees can recognize colors and becomes the first African American to be elected to the St. Louis Academy of Science

1911   Publishes "Experiments in the Pattern Vision of the Honey Bee" in *Biological Bulletin,* showing that bees can recognize patterns

1914   Publishes "Auditory Powers of the Catocala Moths: An Experimental Field Study" and "An Experimental Study of the Auditory Powers of the Giant Silkworm Moths, Saturniidae" in *Biological Bulletin,* proving insects can hear and learn

1922   Becomes ill and retires from Sumner High School

1923   Dies on February 14 in Chicago, Illinois, at age 56

FURTHER READING

Abramson, Charles I. "Charles Henry Turner: Contributions of a Forgotten African-American to Scientific Research." 2003.

Available online. URL: http://psychology.okstate.edu/museum/ turner/turnermain.html. Accessed on January 14, 2005. Extremely useful Web site containing links to a biography, time line, family photographs, and other resources.

————, ed. *Selected Papers and Biography of Charles Henry Turner (1867–1923); Pioneer in the Comparative Animal Behavior Movement.* Lewiston, N.Y.: Edwin Mellen Press, 2003. Most complete resource about the life and works of Turner.

Garraty, John A., and Mark C. Carnes, eds. *American National Biography.* Vol. 22. New York: Oxford University Press, 1999. Brief accounts of the lives and works of famous Americans in encyclopedia format.

Gates, Henry Louis, Jr., and Cornel West. *The African-American Century: How Blacks Have Shaped Our Country.* New York: Touchstone, 2002. Profiles 100 African Americans who made a contribution to science during the 20th century.

Hayden, Robert C. *7 African American Scientists.* Frederick, Md.: Twenty-first Century Books, 1992. Examines the lives and achievements of seven African Americans who made significant contributions to various scientific fields. Appropriate for young adults.

Jenkins, Edward S., ed. *American Black Scientists and Inventors.* Washington, D.C.: National Science Teachers Association, 1975. Describes the background, achievements, and personalities of 12 African-American scientists and inventors.

Krapp, Kristine M., ed. *Notable Black American Scientists.* Detroit: Gale Research, 1999. Brief biographies of approximately 250 black Americans who have made contributions to the sciences.

Sir Alexander Fleming

8

(1881–1955)

Sir Alexander Fleming discovered the antibacterial action of a substance produced by the mold *Penicillium*. (© *The Nobel Foundation*)

The Miracle Drug

When human beings ended their nomadic existence and began living in close proximity to one another, infectious diseases became a major factor in limiting the population size of civilizations. As cities became established, sudden outbreaks of diseases, called *epidemics*, occurred. The bubonic plague, influenza, smallpox, gonorrhea, tuberculosis, malaria, yellow fever, and other infectious diseases decimated populations. People were ignorant and blamed infections on irrelevant factors such as sinful lifestyles. In the late 1800s, the first real advances in fighting infectious diseases were made by the German physician Robert Koch and the French scientist Louis Pasteur. They demonstrated that microorganisms cause diseases, established the means to identify the organisms that cause specific diseases, and developed vaccination as a means to prevent diseases caused by certain microbes. No real progress was made toward fighting infectious diseases once a body was already wracked with infection until the 20th century. Sir Alexander Fleming was a Scottish-born bacteriologist who discovered the *antibacterial* properties of a substance produced by the mold *Penicillium notatum*. This discovery led to a revolution in medicine, stimulating the discovery of several life-saving antimicrobial compounds that destroy *pathogenic* (disease-causing) microbes after they have infected a host.

A Late Start in Medicine

Alexander Fleming was born to Hugh Fleming and his second wife, Grace Morton Fleming, on August 6, 1881, in Lochfield, Ayrshire, Scotland. Nicknamed Alec, he was his father's seventh of eight children and grew up on an 800-acre farm, where he spent his younger days tending the family's sheep, playing in the barns, and fishing in the river. Surrounded by nature, he developed keen observational skills while learning to hunt for peewit eggs and rabbits with his bare hands. He started attending school when he was five, and his father died when he was seven.

At age 13 Alec went to London to live with one of his older brothers who was an eye doctor. Alec took business classes at the Regent Street Polytechnic Institute for two years and by age 16 had passed all of his exams. Not particularly interested in any specific career, he took a job as a junior clerk in a shipping office, where his duties included hand-copying records, bookkeeping, and keeping track of all the cargo and passengers on the ships. In 1900, he joined the London Scottish Regiment, but the Boer War between the United Kingdom and the southern African colonies ended before he was sent overseas. For enjoyment Alec played on the regiment's water polo team and entered shooting competitions, which he often won. He remained a member of the regiment until 1914. His shipping job bored him, so when his uncle left him an inheritance he decided to spend it studying medicine, like his brother.

Fleming was almost 20, older than most embarking on the path to a medical career, but he hired a private tutor and in less than one year passed his exams ahead of all the other British candidates. In October 1901, Fleming entered St. Mary's Hospital Medical School on a scholarship. He chose St. Mary's over the 11 other London medical schools because once he had played against them in water polo. He became enthralled by his studies of anatomy and physiology and excelled with minimum effort while also participating in the school's water polo team, drama society, debate team, and rifle club. In 1906, Fleming received his Conjoint Board Diploma, which granted him permission to practice general medicine, but at the suggestion of one of his teammates, he joined the inoculation department as a junior assistant so he would be eligible to participate as a school team member in an upcoming national rifle competition.

Research on Infections and Inoculations

The inoculation department was headed by Almroth Wright, a staunch believer in *vaccine* therapy. Wright believed in the hope offered by Pasteur's work on vaccines. Vaccines stimulate the body's immune system to produce *antibodies* against disease-causing microbes by the introduction of weakened or killed microbes or parts of the microbes into the body. Antibodies are proteins produced by white blood cells that defend against or help prevent diseases. Some vaccines called toxoids stimulate production of antibodies against a poison produced by a microorganism. Wright was convinced that all infectious diseases could be cured by antibodies either made by the patient or by the introduction of serum from another person. His department extensively examined how vaccinations worked and also studied *phagocytes*. Found in body tissues and fluids, phagocytes are cells that are capable of ingesting and destroying harmful substances or disease-causing microbes. In 1908, Fleming passed his final medical examinations and was awarded the gold medal of the University of London. Though

Fleming was interested in the research, he decided to take the exam necessary to specialize in surgery. He passed the surgical examinations in 1909, but he continued to work for Wright and gained a favorable reputation.

One of Fleming's earliest medical accomplishments was the development of a diagnostic test for *syphilis*, a potentially fatal sexually transmitted disease. German bacteriologist Paul Ehrlich identified a compound effective in treating syphilis, *salvarsan*, in 1910. Fleming became an expert in *intravenously* administering salvarsan to treat syphilis. Intravenous injections were uncommon at the time, and many doctors did not know how to give them.

In 1914, Fleming and several other members of Wright's team joined the Royal Army Medical Corps and established a research center in Boulogne, France. He had to pass through the patient wards on the way to his laboratory, and the surgeons often showed him severe cases of septicemia, tetanus, and other infectious diseases. The number of infections suffered by wounded soldiers and the apparent ineffectiveness of the *antiseptics* used to treat them astounded Fleming. He was particularly horrified by the deadly gas gangrene that caused high fevers, brownish pus at the infection site, and the production of gas below the skin. In these cases, amputation of the infected limbs was necessary in order to save the patient's life. Fleming researched the effect of antiseptics such as carbolic acid, boric acid, and hydrogen peroxide on wounds and found that in the case of deep wounds, these substances actually did more harm than good because the chemicals killed the white blood cells that naturally fight off infection, and they did not penetrate deep enough into the wound to be effective. Wright and Fleming encouraged rinsing wounds with only saline solution and letting the body combat bacterial infections naturally, but most doctors ignored their recommendations.

While on leave in 1915, Fleming married an Irish nurse named Sarah Marion McElroy, whom he called Sareen. In 1921, they bought a country house they called The Dhoon, where they spent weekends together. In 1924, they had one cherished son, Robert, who later became a physician. Sareen died in 1949, and in 1953 Fleming married a Greek bacteriologist, Dr. Amalia Coutsouris-Voureka, who had come to work at St. Mary's in 1946.

Magical Substance in Mucus and Tears

In January 1918, Fleming returned to London and to his studies of bacteriology. His experiences treating wounded soldiers with severe infections motivated him to search for an effective antiseptic. The British physician Joseph Lister founded antiseptic surgery, in which the environment, medical instruments, and surgeons' hands were sterilized before use. This practice, which required instruments to be soaked in carbolic acid to kill any contaminating microorganisms, greatly reduced infection rates following surgeries. However, the acid damaged living tissues. Fleming wanted to find an antiseptic that would not cause harm to the patient's tissues but would effectively kill potential microbial invaders. Meanwhile, Wright appointed Fleming assistant director of the inoculation department, which was renamed the pathology and research department.

Anxious to obtain *cultures* of a wide variety of bacteria, Fleming collected many unusual specimens and grew them in the laboratory in *petri dishes* containing artificial *media*. One interesting sample was obtained from his nasal mucus, collected during a recent cold. The plate had many golden-yellow colonies of the bacteria that he later named *Micrococcus lysodeikticus*. In 1921, while preparing to dispose of the culture dish, he examined it once more and noticed the bacterial colonies immediately surrounding the mucus itself appeared dissolved. He wondered if the mucus contained an antibacterial agent.

Further investigation showed that mucus did indeed contain a substance that naturally killed bacteria. He named it *lysozyme*, since it lysed, or broke open, the bacterial cells. Lysozyme acts by punching holes in the cell walls that encircle bacterial cells. With the integrity of the cell disrupted, the cellular contents leaked out, and the cells perished. After examining many other bodily fluids, Fleming also found lysozyme in tears (collected by squeezing lemon juice into his own eyes and the eyes of others), saliva, blood serum, pus, and egg whites. Lysozyme obviously was not harmful to the host's living tissues or to the host's own immune system components, as were chemical antiseptics. The substance was harmful only to the invading bacteria, acting as a first line of defense to prevent

Growing Bacteria

Bacteria are cheap and easy to maintain in a laboratory environment. They can be grown in either liquid broth or on semisolid media containing sugars, amino acids, vitamins, and other necessary nutrients. Broths are liquid media that are used to grow bacteria in test tubes, flasks, or bottles, which are sometimes shaken during growth in order to aerate the media to provide more oxygen. When sterile, most broths are transparent, and as bacterial growth occurs, the media turn cloudy. Semisolid media are made by the addition of *agar*, a gelatinous substance extracted from algae, to broth. When heated, the agar dissolves, and the media are poured into petri dishes, small circular plates with lids. As they cool, the media solidify, and bacteria can be spread over the surface to grow. If the bacterial culture is diluted sufficiently before plating, then individual bacterial cells divide and multiply, giving rise to single circular-shaped colonies that are usually less than 1/25th of an inch (1 mm) in diameter. Whether bacteria are grown in liquid or solid media, they are incubated at the temperature optimal for the growth of that species. Bacteria that cause diseases in humans usually grow best at 98.6°F (37°C), normal body temperature. When inoculating media with specific bacteria, it is important to maintain a sterile environment so that no undesired contaminating bacteria are accidentally introduced.

bacteria from colonizing the body. He tested microorganisms that were *virulent* to different degrees and, not surprisingly, found that the microbes that were the most susceptible to lysozyme were the least dangerous. Fleming thought this made sense, because if they were not susceptible to lysozyme, they would be more likely to invade the body and cause infection. Fleming was unable to successfully prepare concentrated extracts of lysozyme, but later others were able to crystallize the bacteriolytic enzyme, which has come to be an important tool for microbiologists.

The Wonder Drug

Fleming was noted for his procrastination in cleaning up his old culture dishes, though he was always able to find what he needed among the dozens of stacked plates on his lab bench. This habit resulted in one of the most important medical breakthroughs of the 20th century. A plate with *staphylococci* had become contaminated with a fuzzy-looking mold later identified as *Penicillium notatum*. Staphylococci are spherical-shaped bacteria that grow in clusters, like grapes. Staphylococci may cause infections by entering breaks in the skin that lead to pimples, boils, or a skin disease called impetigo. Though bacteria were found throughout the plate, there were no colonies in the immediate vicinity of the mold. Instead, there was a clear halo surrounding the mold growth. Fleming recognized what none of his colleagues noticed when he showed them the petri dish—that the mold must have been secreting an antibacterial substance. He named it *penicillin*.

Fleming systematically investigated his observation, first by culturing the mold, growing it in the lab, and then trying to duplicate the bactericidal action. He inoculated a plate of agar with the mold at the center and then streaked different bacterial cultures like radii of the circular petri dish. After incubation, some bacteria grew near the mold, while others did not. The mold thrived on a broth containing meat extract, which he poured into sterile bottles and then inoculated with tiny pieces of the mold. He filtered some of the broth in which the mold grew and applied it to plates containing healthy staphylococcal cultures. He performed a series of dilutions to determine the strength necessary to destroy the bacteria and looked for negative effects on living tissue. To see if penicillin was effective in killing other types of bacteria, he added it to plates of several other species. Penicillin proved effective against bacteria that caused pneumonia, syphilis, gonorrhea, diphtheria, and scarlet fever, but not against microorganisms that caused influenza,

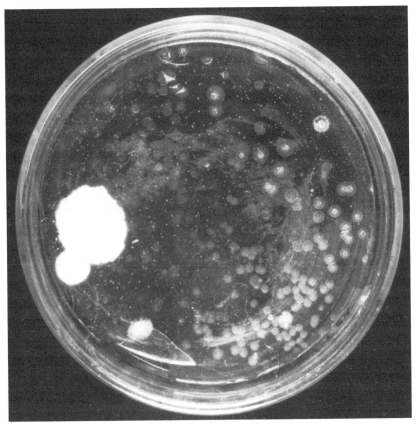

In this photograph of the original culture plate with the contaminating fungus *Penicillium notatum,* the large bright sport is the mold, and the smaller circular shapes are the bacterial colonies. *(St. Mary's Hospital Medical School/Photo Researchers, Inc.)*

whooping cough, typhoid, dysentery, and other intestinal infections. Injection of penicillin into mice and rabbits caused no ill effects.

In 1929, Fleming, now a professor of bacteriology at the University of London, reported that penicillin did not harm white blood cells and elicited no negative responses in laboratory animals. In the paper "On the Antibacterial Action of Cultures of a *Penicillium,* with Special Reference to Their Use in the Isolation of *B. influenzae,*" published in the *British Journal of Experimental Pathology,* Fleming described not only the possible use of penicillin as an injectable antiseptic agent but also a unique application of penicillin, namely in the establishment of pure cultures of other bacteria. Because penicillin was very effective against some bacteria and not at all against others, it could be added to the media used to grow the penicillin-resistant cultures to ensure pure cultures, that is, cultures containing only the desired bacteria.

Fleming and his assistants tried to develop a method for the extraction and concentration of penicillin so they could attempt clinical trials, but it kept losing its potency. By 1932, Fleming stopped actively researching penicillin, but he maintained a culture of *Penicillium* in the laboratory at all times and generously provided specimens to scientists who requested it. In 1935, the German physician Gerhard Domagk announced the identification of the *sulfonamide* prontosil as a cure for systemic *streptococcal* infections, stimulating others to search for additional magic bullets. Fleming switched his focus to the antibacterial properties of sulfonamides, a new class of chemically related drugs found to be effective in preventing the multiplication of some types bacteria, but he maintained his hope that penicillin would one day be an effective treatment for fatal bacterial infections.

Progress at Oxford

The Australian pathologist Sir Howard Florey (1898–1968) and the German biochemist Ernst Chain (1906–79) at Oxford University spent time in the late 1930s characterizing lysozyme. In researching antibacterial substances, they came across Fleming's journal article describing penicillin. By 1940, they successfully developed a procedure involving lyophilization (freeze-drying) and dissolution in methanol for purifying stable penicillin in quantities large enough to test on animals. After a few preliminary investigations, Florey injected 50 white mice with lethal doses of virulent *streptococci*. He then injected penicillin into 25 of those mice at three-hour intervals for two days and nights; the other 25 were not treated. Within 16 hours, the 25 untreated mice were all dead, but 24 of the treated mice survived. These results were published in "Penicillin as a Chemotherapeutic Agent" in the journal *Lancet* in 1940. Fleming was thrilled when he read the article and went to visit Oxford as soon as possible, where the researchers congratulated one another and exchanged information.

The Oxford team performed a series of experiments to determine the best mode of treatment and the optimal dosages. The next step was a human trial, but they needed 3,000 times more penicillin than they used in the mice trial. Thus, they geared up their production methods. They converted every bit of free space to grow massive amounts of *Penicillium*, creating a makeshift factory in the pathology building and using a variety of everyday objects to extract and concentrate the penicillin juice.

Finally, they had enough penicillin. Their first patient was Albert Alexander, a policeman who had scratched his face on a rosebush and as a result developed severe staphylococcal infections covering his head and potentially fatal blood poisoning. Sulfonamides were not effective, and without treatment he was sure to die. On February 12, 1941, they began a series of injections, and he showed marked improvement. Unfortunately, the bacteria began multiplying again, and this time they did not have any more penicillin to give him, so he died. Slowly, they produced enough penicillin to test on several more humans, and in all cases it proved effective.

The Oxford team knew they needed help synthesizing the large quantities of penicillin necessary to treat humans but could not find anybody in Great Britain willing to help them. An agricultural research laboratory in Peoria, Illinois, agreed to grow the mold and extract large quantities of penicillin. However, once the word spread about the miraculous infection-fighting properties that the mold juice possessed, all of the product was devoted to treating war casualties. In 1944, production had ramped enough for civilians to benefit from treatment with penicillin.

In 1942, the director of an optical lens–making business owned by Fleming's older brothers, Harry Lambert, was dying at St. Mary's Hospital from *meningitis*, an infection of the membranes that surround the brain and spinal cord. Fleming removed a sample of

(opposite page) Chain and Florey used a variety of everyday objects to produce penicillin juice in bulk.

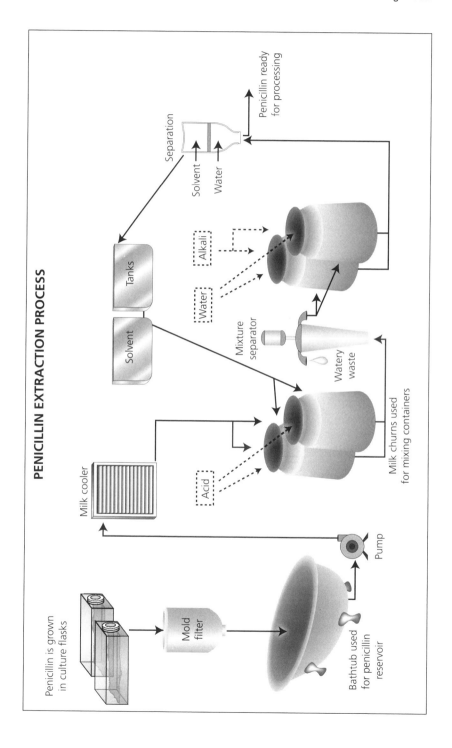

PENICILLIN EXTRACTION PROCESS

Penicillin is grown in culture flasks

Mold filter

Bathtub used for penicillin reservoir

Pump

Milk cooler

Acid

Milk churns used for mixing containers

Solvent

Tanks

Water

Alkali

Mixture separator

Watery waste

Separation

Solvent

Water

Penicillin ready for processing

fluid from Lambert's spinal column and examined it under a micro-scope. He found streptococci. Though doctors had administered sulfonamides to Lambert, he showed no improvement. Fleming wrote Florey to ask for some penicillin, which Florey provided. Every three hours for one day, Fleming injected penicillin into Lambert, and for the first time in six weeks his body temperature returned to normal. When Lambert became feverish again the following week, Fleming took another sample of fluid from his spinal column and once again found streptococci. After consulting with Florey, Fleming decided to directly inject penicillin into Lambert's spinal column. After several injections, Lambert miraculously improved and within one month was completely recovered.

Widespread Fame

By this time, news of the wonder drug was widespread, and Fleming became famous. Several large pharmaceutical firms began researching penicillin production methods. The most respected scientific society in Great Britain, the Royal Society of London, elected Alexander Fleming to membership in 1943, and the following year he was knighted. In 1945, Fleming was awarded the Nobel Prize in physiology or medicine, shared with Chain and Florey, for the discovery of penicillin and its curative effect in various infectious diseases. Other numerous honors and medals were showered upon Fleming such as the Moxon Medal from the Royal College of Physicians, the Honorary Gold Medal of the Royal College of Surgeons (1946), the Gold Medal of the Royal Society of Medicine (1947), and the Medal for Merit from the United States of America (1947). He spent much of his time traveling around the world making appearances, giving speeches, and accepting almost 30 honorary degrees from European and American universities.

Sir Alexander Fleming died following a heart attack on March 11, 1955, in London, England. The shaggy-haired man who was known for wearing bowties and playing snooker at the Chelsea Arts Club in the evenings was buried in St. Paul's Cathedral. He had never received any money for his hard work and discovery; he donated it all to St. Mary's for research. Today the Wright-Fleming Institute at the Imperial College London, named in tribute to Fleming and his mentor, houses scientists dedicated to researching human bacterial and viral infections. Often serendipity is credited for the discovery that launched a medical revolution, but one must remember the man who took notice, believed, and pursued what he observed.

Fleming devoted his life to helping humanity by trying to figure out how to fight infections. He did not invent penicillin, and, in fact, was not the first to discover it, as others before him had noticed that mold had some antibacterial properties, but Fleming was the first to recognize its broad significance and to draw attention to it. Since Fleming discovered the *antibiotic* penicillin, hundreds of other chemicals naturally produced by microorganisms have been found to have antibacterial properties. Interestingly, Fleming prophetically warned against the improper use of antibiotics, predicting it would lead to antibiotic resistance. Insufficient doses, not completing the entire course of an antibiotic treatment, and the widespread use of antibiotics for cattle as well as the use of antibiotics to treat colds and other nonbacterial maladies has resulted in a sharp increase in the number of strains of bacteria that are resistant to a wide variety of antibiotics, the result of which is the need for another Sir Alexander Fleming.

CHRONOLOGY

1881   Alexander Fleming is born on August 6 at Lochfield, Ayrshire, Scotland

1895   Enrolls at the Regent Street Polytechnic Institute in London

1897   Starts job in London as a shipping clerk

1900–14 Serves in the London Scottish Rifle Volunteers

1901   Enters St. Mary's Hospital Medical School in London

1906   Passes medical school exams and joins Almroth Wright's inoculation department at St. Mary's Hospital

1909   Passes surgical specialty examinations but continues working in the inoculation department at St. Mary's

1914–18 Serves in the Royal Army Medical Corps in Boulogne, France, during World War I

1921	Discovers the bacteriolytic substance lysozyme and becomes assistant director of inoculation department at St. Mary's Hospital in London
1922	Publishes first lysozyme paper, "On a Remarkable Bacteriolytic Element Found in Tissues and Secretions" in *Proceedings of the Royal Society of London*
1928	Discovers antibacterial properties of penicillin and is appointed professor of bacteriology at the University of London
1929	Publishes first penicillin paper, "On the Antibacterial Action of Cultures of a *Penicillium* with Special Reference to Their Use in the Isolation of *B. influenzae*" in the *British Journal of Experimental Pathology*
1940	Ernst Chain and Howard Florey extract enough penicillin to inject into mice
1941	Albert Alexander becomes the first human to be injected with penicillin purified by Florey and Chain. He shows improvement but then dies because there is not enough penicillin to continue treatment
1942	Fleming injects penicillin directly into the spinal fluid of Harry Lambert, who completely recovers
1944	Fleming is knighted for his discovery of penicillin and is elected a fellow of the Royal College of Physicians
1945	Fleming, Chain, and Florey are awarded the Nobel Prize in physiology or medicine for the discovery of penicillin and its curative effect in various infectious diseases
1946	Becomes director of the inoculation department at St. Mary's Hospital upon Wright's retirement
1948	Becomes emeritus professor of bacteriology, University of London, but retains directorship of inoculation department until his death
1955	Dies on March 11 following a heart attack at age 73 in London, England

FURTHER READING

Birch, Beverley. *Alexander Fleming: Pioneer with Antibiotics.* Detroit: Blackbirch Press, 2002. Part of the *Giants of Science* series that reveals how the minds of great scientists were prepared. Written for juvenile readers.

Gillispie, Charles C., ed. *Dictionary of Scientific Biography.* Vol. 5. New York: Scribner, 1970–76. Good source for facts concerning personal backgrounds and scientific accomplishments but assumes reader has basic knowledge of science.

Horvitz, Leslie Alan. *Eureka! Scientific Breakthroughs that Changed the World.* New York: John Wiley, 2002. Explores the events and thought processes that led 12 great minds to their eureka moments.

Macfarlane, Gwyn. *Alexander Fleming: The Man and the Myth.* Cambridge, Mass.: Harvard University Press, 1984. Full-length biography of Fleming written for adults.

Nobelprize.org. "The Nobel Prize in Physiology or Medicine 1945." Available online. URL: http://www.nobelprize.org/medicine/laureates/1945. Last modified June 16, 2000. Includes links to Fleming's biography and Nobel lecture as well as those of Ernst Boris Chain and Sir Howard Walter Florey.

9

Rita Levi-Montalcini

(1909–   )

Rita Levi-Montalcini discovered nerve
growth factor, a crucial protein in the
development of the nervous system.
(© The Nobel Foundation)

The Discovery of Nerve Growth Factor

The transformation of a single fertilized egg cell into the tens of
trillions of cells that constitute an adult human being is a mysterious and remarkable process. The zygote first undergoes several
rounds of cell division, and then the cells begin to diverge struc-
turally and functionally as they become specialized in a process
called *differentiation*. What directs the embryo's cellular activities?
How does each cell know what to do and when to do it? Little was
known about the molecular mechanisms of development 50 years

ago when the work of a dedicated Italian researcher who began her career in a homemade laboratory revealed a chemical substance with extraordinary powers. Rita Levi-Montalcini discovered *nerve growth factor* (NGF), a protein produced by the body that controls the growth of neurons and is required for their survival. Decades later, scientists are learning the implications of NGF in cancer treatment, Alzheimer's disease management, birth defects, and research in other fields.

Desire for a Professional Career

Rita Levi and her fraternal twin sister, Paola, were born on April 22, 1909, in Turin, Italy, to an intellectual Jewish family. Her father, Adamo Levi, was an electrical engineer and a factory manager, and her mother, Adele Montalcini Levi, was a talented painter. The twin girls grew up with their older sister and brother in a loving but traditional home where the father was the undisputed, authoritarian head of the family. He did not believe girls needed a university education to fulfill their intended roles as wives and mothers, so even though Rita was very bright, he enrolled her at a less academically rigorous girls' finishing school. When her former governess was diagnosed with stomach cancer, the previously submissive 20-year-old Rita resolved to become a physician. Realizing she could never be happy without pursuing a professional career, she convinced her father to grant her permission and worked diligently to compensate for her limited educational preparation. Within eight months she learned Latin, Greek, and mathematics, graduated from high school, and entered medical school at the University of Turin, where she took classes from the famous histologist Dr. Giuseppe Levi (no relation).

As an adult, Levi added her mother's maiden name to her own in order to distinguish herself from other Levis from Turin, becoming Rita Levi-Montalcini. She graduated summa cum laude in 1936 but was not sure if she wanted to practice medicine or become a medical researcher, so she began investigating the nervous system as Levi's research assistant. He taught her a sensitive new technique for staining neurons of chick embryos using chrome silver. In 1938, she was forced to resign as a result of a racial manifesto issued by the Italian fascist dictator Benito Mussolini that prohibited Jews from holding academic or other professional positions. She left the country to work at the Neurological Institute in Brussels, Belgium, until December 1939, right before the German army invaded Belgium.

Clandestine Investigations

Back in Turin, Levi-Montalcini set up a secret research laboratory in her home, using a small binocular microscope, a *stereomicroscope* for operating on embryos, an incubator that her brother made, and primitive dissecting tools including watchmaker's forceps, tiny oph- thalmologic scissors, and scalpels and spatulas ground from com- mon sewing needles. She begged farmers for fertilized eggs (claiming they would be more nutritious for her fictitious children) and found solace from the distress of war by immersing herself in the development of the nervous system in chick embryos. Her for- mer mentor, Giuseppe Levi, fled to Turin from Belgium and joined her. Levi-Montalcini had read an article by Viktor Hamburger, a German-born *neuroembryologist* (one who studies the development of the nervous system in unborn animals) who was working in America. Hamburger performed experiments that revealed that destruction of limb buds in chick embryos greatly reduced the growth of nerves to the limb buds. He hypothesized that the absence of an inductive factor released by innervated tissues pre- vented the growth of *motor neurons* (nerve cells that transmit signals from the brain or spinal cord to muscles) and *sensory neurons* (nerve cells that receive information and transmit signals to the central nervous system).

Intrigued by what influenced the formation and differentiation of the embryonic nerves, Levi-Montalcini repeated the experi- ments Hamburger described by amputating limb buds from chick embryos and observing the effects on the nerves growing from the spinal cord. After various periods of time, she sliced thin sec- tions of the spinal cord, silver-stained them, and examined them under her microscope. She found that in the absence of a limb, the motor neurons leading to that limb disappeared. Whereas

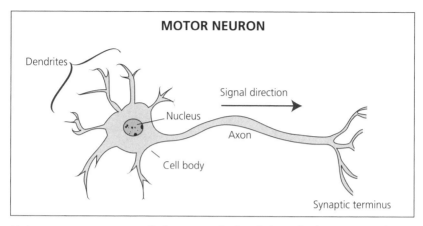

MOTOR NEURON

Dendrites

Signal direction

Nucleus

Axon

Cell body

Synaptic terminus

Motor neurons are nerve cells that transmit signals from the brain or spinal cord to muscles or glands.

Hamburger believed they were never induced to grow in the first place, Levi-Montalcini's careful observations led her to believe that the motor and sensory neurons did grow, but then they died. She thought that after *proliferation* and differentiation began, a factor released by the limb buds stimulated continued growth and development. The absence of such a factor led to degeneration. Unable to publish the results in Italian journals because of the manifesto banning Jews from performing academic research, Levi-Montalcini and Levi eventually published them in Belgian and Swiss journals.

Systematic bombing of Turin by Allied forces in 1942 forced Levi-Montalcini to relocate her home laboratory to the countryside. The threats from the war were too dangerous for her to carry on her forbidden studies, and less than two years later she fled to Florence, where she lived under a false identity. After the Nazis lost control of the city in 1944, she worked as a volunteer physician for the Allied forces at a refugee camp for the duration of the war.

A Signal for Neuron Growth

After the war ended in 1945, Levi-Montalcini resumed her position as Levi's laboratory assistant at the University of Turin. In 1946, she received an invitation from Hamburger, who had read her research articles, to enter a collaborative research project on the regulation of chick embryonic development at Washington University in St. Louis, Missouri. The research Levi-Montalcini conducted in her private home laboratory during the war had been inspired by the work of Hamburger, yet they had formulated different conclusions to explain their observations. He believed that tissues and organs in the body sent out signals inducing cells of the developing nervous system to grow and divide. Without the limb, the motor neurons did not receive a signal to proliferate. Levi-Montalcini thought a specific nutrient was needed for already-proliferating nerves to survive and to continue growing. Despite their competing ideas and different approaches, the two developed a friendly working relationship. She planned to stay for less than one year, but the success of their joint research persuaded her to stay for three decades. Washington University named her an associate professor of zoology in 1956 and a full professor in 1958.

Levi-Montalcini continued to research development of the nervous system in chick embryos and demonstrated that a specific factor was necessary for normal nerve cell growth and differentiation, as she had hypothesized. By scrutinizing microscope slides of sections taken from various stages of development, she reconstructed the process step by step, counting new nerve cells and noting their locations. In 1947, she finally recognized the big picture, involving the programmed migration of nerve cells to predetermined destinations and then the demise and removal of certain cells by the embryonic immune system. Neurons degenerated in the course of normal development, not only following the ablation of a limb bud, and the evidence of their previous existence was quickly cleaned up. Her intuition told her that a factor or hormone made in the limbs acted as a feedback signal necessary to sustain the growth of new neurons.

Tumors, Snake Venom, and Salivary Glands

In the 1950s, at Hamburger's suggestion, Levi-Montalcini surgically attached fragments of mouse tumors to chicken embryos and was elated to observe nerve fibers chaotically growing on, all around, and into the tumors. She surmised that the tumors produced and released a potent chemical *growth factor*, a substance that stimulates cell growth. When she attached the tumor to an external membrane that was connected to the embryo only through blood circulation, the nerves still grew, demonstrating that the signaling factor was not conveyed along nervous pathways but was a *humoral* factor, meaning it was transported by the blood.

A friend from medical school named Hertha Meyer had fled to Rio de Janeiro during the war and was an expert at *in vitro* tissue culture. In vitro experiments are performed on tissue growing in glass or plastic dishes in the laboratory rather than in animals and are useful because a scientist has more control over the experimental conditions, and fewer unknown factors complicate interpretation of the results. Using such a technique would speed up Levi-Montalcini's experiments and help her to verify definitively the presence and role of a nerve growth factor, NGF. She smuggled two tumor-laden mice through customs in her coat pocket and visited the Institute of Biophysics in Brazil from 1952 to 1953. In her friend's laboratory, Levi-Montalcini put a piece of the mouse tumor near to, but not touching, a bit of chicken nerve tissue. Within a few hours, dense halo-shaped growths of nerve fibers appeared around the chicken tissue, radiating outward from it like rays from the sun, confirming that a humoral factor secreted by the tumor acted upon the nerve tissue. When she allowed the culture to grow for two or three days, she noticed the new nerves elongated in the direction toward the tumor tissue.

After returning to St. Louis, Levi-Montalcini paired up with an American postdoctoral biochemist, Stanley Cohen (b. 1922), to isolate the growth factor. Levi-Montalcini spent an impatient year growing enough mouse tumors for Cohen to extract a large enough quantity of the factor for identification. Future Nobel laureate (physiology or medicine, 1959) Arthur Kornberg, a biochemist who was working at Washington University at the time, recommended that they purify their fractions by using snake venom to remove excess nucleic acids. Fractions treated with the snake venom turned out to be powerful stimulators of halo formation, suggesting that the venom either neutralized an inhibitor in the tumor extract or

Nerve Growth Factor Action and Promise

As scientists realized the importance of NGF in the 1980s, they reviewed Rita Levi-Montalcini's research from three decades earlier, leading to her nomination for the Nobel Prize in physiology or medicine in 1986. Since her discovery in the early 1950s, medical researchers have learned a great deal concerning NGF's mechanism of action and potential significance. NGF belongs to the *neurotrophin* family of proteins, which induce proliferation and survival of neurons. After secretion, the protein seeks out specific *receptors,* molecules located on the surface of cells that recognize and bind NGF. Only certain cells called target cells have the specific receptors for NGF and react to its presence. Binding of NGF to its receptor triggers a series of biochemical changes within the cell that lead to activation of proteins that induce the nerve cells to grow *axons.* When a growing axon reaches a target cell, a *synapse* is formed, allowing the nerve cell to communicate with the target through the release of *neurotransmitters,* chemical messengers released by one neuron that diffuse across the synapse and bind to specific receptors on a postsynaptic cell.

that it contained a factor with properties similar to the growth factor they were investigating. The latter proved true; astonishingly, the snake venom was 3,000 times richer in NGF than the tumor extract. This accidental discovery led them to purify NGF from mouse salivary glands, correctly thinking that because salivary glands are the mammalian counterpart to the snake glands, they might also be a rich source. With a cheap and abundant supply, Cohen successfully isolated NGF, identified it as a protein (a molecule made up of amino acids), and determined its molecular weight and other physicochemical characteristics.

In 1971, Levi-Montalcini's postdoctoral fellow Ruth Hogue Angeletti and a biochemist named Ralph Bradshaw at Washington University determined the amino acid sequence for NGF. The gene that encodes NGF was identified and sequenced in 1983, enabling the protein to be synthesized using biotechnological methods and its uses to be explored more easily. Damage to nerve tissue, whether caused by injury from stroke, trauma, disease, or aging, is particularly dangerous, since the body has natural mechanisms for inhibiting the regeneration of nervous tissue, such as molecules that inhibit the growth of axons. Medical researchers currently are investigating treatments using NGF for brain and spinal cord injuries and neurodegenerative diseases such as Alzheimer's, Lou Gehrig's, and Parkinson's. At the American Academy of Neurology meeting in 2004, Dr. Mark Tuszynski and colleagues from the University of California at San Diego reported that grafting skin cells that had been genetically modified to produce NGF into the brains of people with early Alzheimer's delayed brain cell loss and increased cellular activity. Another promising study presented by Gary Hotton and colleagues from Imperial College London showed that infusion of a neurotrophic factor directly into the brains of Parkinson's patients reduced symptoms by 40 percent.

Over a six-year period, Levi-Montalcini characterized NGF with respect to its biological properties, while Cohen analyzed its chemical properties. Injection of NGF into newborn rodents induced the formation of many new neurons. Using immunological techniques, they showed that NGF was important in the differentiation and survival of certain types of nerve cells. Antiserum to snake venom inhibited the in vitro formation of the fibrillar halos. They made NGF-specific antibodies, proteins manufactured by the immune system that recognize and bind to specific molecules, and the specific antibodies also prevented the formation of the halos. When injected into newborn rodents, the NGF-specific antibodies bound to the natural NGF that was present, and the developing nerves suffered almost complete atrophy.

Due to budget constraints at Washington University, Hamburger could not offer Cohen a permanent position. In 1959, Cohen left for Vanderbilt University, and an Italian named Piero Angeletti assisted Levi-Montalcini in investigations on the structure of NGF.

Home Again

In 1961, Levi-Montalcini returned to Italy, and with the help of Piero Angeletti, she established a laboratory at the Higher Institute of Health in Rome, where she continued performing neurobiological research. The Italian National Research Council (CNR) transformed her research unit into the Institute of Cell Biology in 1969. She spent half of each year in Italy and the other half in the United States until 1977, when she retired from Washington University and became a professor emerita. She retired as director of the Laboratory of Cell Biology in 1979 and became a guest professor at the CNR's Institute of Neurobiology in Rome and a guest researcher at the Institute of Cell Biology.

Levi-Montalcini joined numerous scientific organizations including the American Academy of Arts and Sciences, the Belgian Royal Academy of Medicine, the National Academy of Sciences of Italy, the European Academy of Sciences, Arts, and Letters, and the Academy of Arts and Sciences of Florence. In 1968, the National Academy of Sciences elected her a member, only the 10th woman elected since its foundation in 1863. In 1974, she became the first female member of the Pontifical Academy of Sciences in Rome. She has been honored many times, and in 1986 she received the highly regarded Nobel Prize in physiology or medicine, shared with Stanley Cohen, for their discovery of growth factors. In 1987, President Ronald Reagan awarded her the highest distinction bestowed upon American scientists, the National Medal of Science. Several universities, including the University of London and Harvard University, have granted her honorary degrees, and she has declined many more.

Levi-Montalcini's groundbreaking research on neuroembryonic development revealed an important clue to the mystery of cellular growth and differentiation. Since her discovery of NGF in 1952, scientists have identified and studied numerous other factors that perform similar functions in a variety of cell and tissue types. In addition to pioneering a molecular movement in developmental biology, the discovery of NGF has led to many new effective treatments for a variety of maladies. Therapeutic use of NGF to slow the progression of neurodegenerative diseases or to stimulate the growth of motor neurons in spinal cord injury patients may be among the most optimistic goals, but NGF has also been effective in speeding healing from burns, diminishing the negative effects of chemotherapy and radiation therapy, healing bedsores, and eradicating corneal ulcers.

CHRONOLOGY

1909   Rita Levi-Montalcini is born on April 22 in Turin, Italy

1936   Earns medical degree from the University of Turin

1936–38 Works as research assistant to Giuseppe Levi at the University of Turin

1939   Works at the Neurological Institute in Brussels, Belgium

1940–43 Secretly researches the development of chick embryos in her home

1943–44 Lives in hiding in Florence, Italy

1944–45 Ministers to war refugees for the Allied health service

1945   Resumes research with Levi

1946–52 Conducts research leading to the discovery of nerve growth factor (NGF) at Washington University in St. Louis

1952–53 Visits the Institute of Biophysics in Rio de Janeiro, Brazil, to perform in vitro experiments

1953–59 Collaborates with Stanley Cohen at Washington University to isolate, identify, and characterize NGF

1956 Becomes associate professor of zoology at Washington University

1958 Becomes full professor at Washington University

1962–69 Establishes a research unit at the Higher Institute of Health in Rome, Italy

1969–78 Directs the Institute of Cell Biology of the Italian National Council of Research in Rome and becomes guest professor upon retirement

1977 Washington University names Levi-Montalcini a professor emerita

1986 Shares the Nobel Prize in physiology or medicine with Cohen for their discoveries of growth factors

1987 Receives the National Medal of Science

FURTHER READING

Dash, Joan. *The Triumph of Discovery: Women Scientists Who Won the Nobel Prize.* Englewood Cliffs, N.J.: Julian Messner, 1991. Stories of the early struggles and breakthroughs of 10 women scientists who were awarded the Nobel Prize.

Encyclopedia of World Biography, Second Edition. Vol. 9. Detroit: Gale Research, 1998. Brief biographies of notable figures and summaries of their accomplishments. Written for high school students.

Levi-Montalcini, Rita. *In Praise of Imperfection: My Life and Work.* New York: Basic Books, 1988. Fascinating full-length autobiography written for nonscientists.

McGrayne, Sharon Bertsch. *Nobel Prize Women in Science.* Washington, D.C.: Joseph Henry Press, 1998. Examines the lives and achievements of 15 women who either won a Nobel Prize or played a crucial role in a Nobel Prize–winning project.

Moritz, Charles, ed. *Current Biography Yearbook 1989.* New York: H. W. Wilson, 1990. Brief biographies of worldwide newsmakers.

Nobelprize.org. "The Nobel Prize in Physiology or Medicine 1986." Available online. URL: http://www.nobelprize.org/medicine/ laureates/1986. Last modified June 16, 2000. Includes links to Levi-Montalcini's and Stanley Cohen's autobiographies and Nobel lectures.

10

James D. Watson

(1928–)

James D. Watson codiscovered the molecular structure of DNA, leading to a revolution in molecular biology. (© *The Nobel Foundation*)

The Double Helical Structure of DNA

Human beings are made up of approximately 10 trillion cells, with each one containing about three feet (about 1 m) of threadlike DNA, the archive of life's secrets, coiled up and packed into a nucleus less than one–ten thousandth of an inch (less than 1μ) in diameter. In 1865, Austrian monk Gregor Mendel described the concept of the gene, but it was not until the 1940s that Oswald Avery and his colleagues demonstrated that *deoxyribonucleic acid*

(DNA) had the ability to confer hereditary characteristics to a cell. During the decade that followed, scientists everywhere scrambled to learn more about this intriguing molecule, including its structure. Two relatively unknown scientists sparked a revolution in biology when they discovered the double helical model for DNA in 1953. James D. Watson and Francis Crick (1916–2004) gave birth to the field of molecular biology when they unraveled the underlying processes of life. The structure immediately revealed a mechanism for its replication and implied that a code must be embedded within the DNA for the synthesis of proteins. These matters had been major mysteries in biology, and surprisingly, one of the men responsible, Watson, was a barely 25-year-old postdoctoral student who had been struggling to find a suitable and interesting research project less than a year before.

A Typical Midwestern Beginning

James Dewey Watson was born on April 6, 1928, in Chicago, Illinois, to James Dewey and Jean Mitchell Watson. He attended the public school system and graduated ahead of his peers. The child prodigy enrolled at the University of Chicago when he was only 15 years old, and though he considered majoring in *ornithology* (the study of birds), he earned his bachelor's degree in zoology in 1947. At Indiana University in Bloomington, he researched the effects of X-rays on the multiplication of *bacteriophage* (a virus that infects bacteria) for his doctoral dissertation and earned a Ph.D. in zoology in 1950.

Having developed a deep interest in genetics while at Indiana University, he applied for and was awarded a fellowship through the National Research Council to study nucleic acid chemistry and virus reproduction at the University of Copenhagen in Denmark with biochemist Herman Kalckar. In May 1951, Watson attended a meeting on the structure of biological macromolecules in Naples, where Maurice H. F. Wilkins (1916–2004), a New Zealand– born *biophysicist* who worked at the Medical Research Council Biophysics Unit at King's College of the University of London, shared X-ray diffraction patterns from crystallized DNA suggesting that it

Francis Crick shared the Nobel Prize in physiology or medicine with James D. Watson and Maurice Wilkins for their discoveries of the structure of nucleic acids. (© *The Nobel Foundation*)

had a regular, highly organized structure that could be resolved within a few years. That same year, Watson moved to Cambridge University, where he accepted an appointment at the Cavendish Laboratory to work with the English chemist John Kendrew on the three-dimensional structure of the oxygen-carrying muscle protein *myoglobin*. There he met the loquacious Francis Crick, an English scientist who studied protein structure for the Medical Research Council Unit for the Study of Molecular Structure of Biological Systems at the Cavendish Laboratory. Crick, who did not earn a Ph.D. until 1954, was an intuitive thinker whose incessant chatter irritated his coworkers. Watson and Crick quickly discovered they had much in common, including an intense desire to be the first to solve the mystery of DNA's structure.

The Puzzle Pieces

Only bits of information were already known regarding DNA. The basic building blocks were called nucleotides, and they consisted of a sugar portion called deoxyribose, a negatively charged phosphate group, and one of four different organic bases that appeared in different proportions in different species. Two of the bases, *cytosine* and *thymine*, were classified as *pyrimidines* and contained a single ring made of nitrogen and carbon atoms. The other two, *adenine* and *guanine*, were called *purines* and had two fused rings as their base.

The width of a DNA molecule was thicker than a single polynucleotide chain. The Czech-American biochemist Erwin Chargaff determined that although different organisms had different

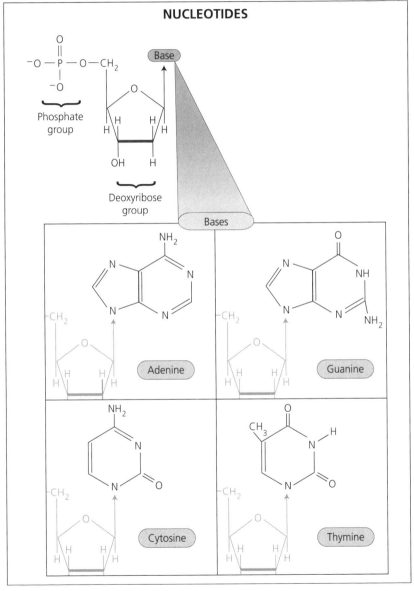

DNA is a polymer made up of four basic building blocks, each consisting of a deoxyribose sugar, a phosphate group, and one of four nitrogenous bases.

amounts of DNA, the percent composition of the base adenine equaled the percent composition of the base thymine, and likewise, the percent composition of cytosine equaled the percent composition of guanine. This information suggested that the bases, which were known to be positioned at right angles to the sugar-phosphate chain, existed in pairs—adenine with thymine and cytosine with guanine. The American biochemist Linus Pauling (1901–94) had recently discovered the alpha-helix, a beautiful spiral structure found in proteins, and some believed DNA might also be helical.

The X-ray diffraction pattern of crystalline DNA that Wilkins had presented in Naples excited Watson about DNA structure. *X-ray crystallography* is a technique often used by biochemists to gather information on the structure of molecules. Diffraction is the bending of waves as they pass by an obstacle, in this case, atoms of the molecules of DNA. Because atoms are much smaller than the wavelengths of visible light, they cannot diffract the light rays or be seen, even with microscopes. The wavelengths of X-rays are much smaller and thus can be used to "see" atoms and molecules. The substance to be x-rayed must first be crystallized, a procedure in which the molecules become highly ordered, with regular spacing occurring between atoms in the arranged molecules. When bombarded with X-rays, the crystallized molecules diffract the waves, which pass through the created spaces as through a grating, forming a unique pattern of blurry circles on photographic film. Wilkins's X-ray diffraction photographs showed that DNA's structure was regular, and therefore solving it was a reasonable expectation.

The physical chemist Rosalind Franklin was a skilled X-ray crystallographer who worked at King's College London with Wilkins, though they did not get along. Watson attended a lecture on different forms of DNA given by her in November 1951. He had prepared for her presentation by teaching himself the principles of X-ray crystallography and was excited by her presentation despite his limited knowledge. He annoyed Crick by not taking lecture notes and not clearly remembering the details of her research, in particular, the water content of the DNA samples she had crystallized. What he did remember, however, seemed to justify the possibility that DNA was helical.

The Ruthless Race

Watson ordered a set of stick and ball models of individual nucleotides from the Cavendish machine shop and impatiently awaited their construction. He felt that building physical models of possible DNA molecules was the best approach for combining all the bits of known information about its structure. Watson tinkered with his nucleotide model pieces, making adjustment after adjustment, continually asking himself whether his creation met the established criteria for the molecule of heredity. Near the end of 1951, Watson and Crick had fashioned a triple-helical model with the sugar-phosphate chain running down the center and the organic bases pointing outward. They anxiously invited Wilkins and Franklin to view their masterpiece, but instead of receiving anticipated praise, they were ridiculed for an unsatisfactory effort that contained 10 times less water than must exist in the correct model. The head of the laboratory, Sir Lawrence Bragg, ordered Watson and Crick to give up their work on DNA, reminding them that the project belonged to the group at King's by priority anyhow. They hesitantly complied, or so it appeared.

Watson worked on tobacco mosaic virus (TMV) structure, but he and Crick could not simply forget what had become their passion. They continued to pay attention to new circulating information about DNA structure, including a report describing the linkage between the sugar of one nucleotide and the phosphate of another nucleotide. Crick took it upon himself to learn more about *hydrogen bonds*, the type of chemical bond now known to hold together two strands of DNA in a double helix. Watson learned more about theoretical chemistry and improved his understanding of the interpretation of X-ray diffraction data. He even obtained his own photographic evidence suggesting that TMV was helical.

Across the Atlantic Ocean, Pauling was soon to win the Nobel Prize (chemistry, 1954) for his research on chemical bonding and its application to the elucidation of the structure of complex substances. He was a front-runner in the competition to solve the structure of DNA, and coincidentally, his son came to the Cavendish Laboratory as a graduate student of Kendrew in the fall of 1952. Peter Pauling received a manuscript written and forwarded by his father in February 1953, before it was published, claiming DNA was a triple helix with the sugar-phosphate backbone in the center. Linus Pauling also had foolishly added hydrogen atoms to the phosphate groups and made them integral to the binding together of the three chains. Adding the hydrogen atoms eliminated

Rosalind Franklin
(1920–1958)

Rosalind Franklin was an expert X-ray crystallographer whom Watson depicted as a belligerent, surly, unsociable feminist. From another perspective, she was an honest, dedicated, unappreciated, talented researcher who fell victim to the sexism that was rampant in the 20th-century world of science.

Born on July 25, 1920, Franklin was the daughter of Jewish socialist parents who lived in London. She excelled at science, graduated from Cambridge in 1941, and began graduate studies in gas-phase chromatography at Newnham College, Cambridge. Unable to get along with her adviser, she quit and took a job as an assistant research officer for the British Coal Utilization Association, studying the physical and chemical properties of coal. She submitted a thesis to Cambridge University on this work, and in 1945 she received a doctorate degree in physical chemistry. The following year she moved to Paris to work for the Laboratoire Central des Services Chimiques de l'État, where she became proficient in X-ray crystallography. At the same time that James Watson became a member of the Cavendish Laboratory, Franklin joined Sir John T. Randall's Medical Research Council Unit at King's College in London, where she used her X-ray diffraction skills with hopes of solving the structure of DNA.

Maurice Wilkins and Franklin initially collaborated to study X-ray fibers obtained from a Swiss lab. Franklin considered herself an equal,

DNA's net charge, yet abounding evidence showed it was an acid. This mistake probably lost Pauling the race, but Watson became worried that Pauling would soon recover from his error and come up with a better model. Bragg, who resented Pauling for unrelated reasons, gave Watson permission to resume work on DNA and

---

but Wilkins treated her more like an assistant, and bare tolerance of each other grew into open hostility. They shared a common research goal, but they eventually stopped sharing information. Though they might have made a formidable team in the race to solve the structure of DNA, their bitter relationship hindered any progress. She publicly denied a helical form for DNA, but her personal laboratory notes divulge she believed otherwise.

When she learned that Watson and Crick planned to publish their model for DNA structure, she and the graduate student Raymond Gosling quickly composed an accompanying article, "Molecular Configuration in Sodium Thymonucleate," published in the same issue of *Nature*, which provided experimental evidence for the double helical model with an exterior phosphate backbone. In July 1953, Franklin and Gosling published another paper in *Nature* detailing the differences between two different forms of DNA, "Evidence for 2-Chain Helix in Crystalline Structure of Sodium Deoxyribonucleate."

After the reports were published, Franklin transferred to J. D. Bernal's laboratory at Birkbeck College London, where she switched the focus of her research to the structure of tobacco mosaic virus, a field to which she made significant contributions. Because she died from ovarian cancer on April 16, 1958, she was not eligible for nomination of the 1962 Nobel Prize for her role in the discovery of DNA structure. How the prize might have been divided is unknown, as the rules also preclude more than three individuals from sharing a given prize. Records of the Nobel archives are released 50 years after a prize is awarded, so in 2008, whether or not she ever was nominated for a Nobel Prize during her lifetime will become known.

encouraged collaboration with the King's team. Watson rushed to King's College to warn Franklin about Pauling's work and try to convince her that the model-building approach would help them solve the structure more quickly, but she brushed him aside and emphatically declared that there was not any data to suggest DNA was helical. Annoyed at Franklin's lack of collegiality and willingness to cooperate, Wilkins later shared with Watson convincing X-ray diffraction photographic evidence that DNA was helical.

The Finish Line and Beyond

Watson and Crick frantically resumed their attempts to reconstruct DNA with nucleotide models. By the end of February, they had discovered the beautiful three-dimensional structure of DNA. Their model was consistent with experimental data found in a report written by Franklin for a committee reviewing work in Randall's lab and unknowingly provided to Watson and Crick. In March 1953, Watson and Crick published their 900-word landmark paper, "A Structure for Deoxyribose Nucleic Acid," in the journal *Nature*. That May they published a second related article speculating on the implications of their described structure on DNA replication, "Genetical Implications of the Structure of Deoxyribonucleic Acid," also in *Nature*.

They deduced that DNA consisted of two parallel, intertwined helical strands. The two polynucleotide strands were *complementary*, meaning each strand contained a sequence of bases that were paired in a specific manner with bases on the other strand; adenine formed hydrogen bonds with thymine, and guanine formed hydrogen bonds with cytosine. The outer portion of each strand consisted of a chain of alternating sugars and phosphate groups, and the inner portion consisted of the paired bases. If the spiral helix were unwound, the structure resembled a ladder, with the sides of the ladder representing the parallel sugar-phosphate backbones and the rungs representing the paired bases.

The structure implied a simple mechanism for duplicating the genetic material prior to cell division. Separation of the two strands by pulling apart the hydrogen bonds between paired bases would allow the DNA replication machinery to insert complementary

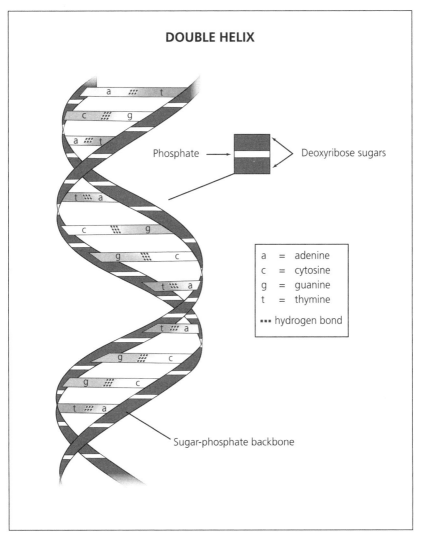

DOUBLE HELIX

Phosphate ⟶

Deoxyribose sugars

a = adenine
c = cytosine
g = guanine
t = thymine

••• hydrogen bond

Sugar-phosphate backbone

The double helical model proposed that two strands of DNA were wound spirally around each other and connected by complementary base-pairing. Adenine specifically pairs with guanine through the formation of two hydrogen bonds, and cytosine pairs with thymine by forming three hydrogen bonds.

nucleotides, creating two new DNA molecules that were identical to each other and to the original molecule. The sequence of the bases along a strand encoded for the proteins act as building blocks and as the molecular workhorses of the cell.

After attending a symposium on viruses in June 1953 at Cold Spring Harbor Laboratory (CSHL) on Long Island, New York, Watson accepted a position as a senior research fellow in biology at the California Institute of Technology, where he carried out X-ray diffraction studies of RNA until 1955. He returned to the Cavendish Laboratory to collaborate further with Crick on virus construction for one year before joining the faculty at Harvard University, where he remained until 1976. In hopes of being able to elucidate the mechanisms of protein synthesis, he researched ribonucleic acid, which is similar in structure to DNA.

In 1962, Watson, Crick, and Wilkins were awarded the Nobel Prize in physiology or medicine for their discoveries concerning the molecular structure of nucleic acids and their significance for information transfer in living material. Though Franklin's data were crucial to the structure's elucidation, Nobel recipients must be living at the time of the nomination, and she had passed away in 1958.

Watson wrote the first molecular biology textbook, *Molecular Biology of the Gene*, in 1965. The book is currently in its fifth edition. Three years later, Watson published *The Double Helix*, an informal personal account of the intense process and chaotic series of events that led to the discovery of the structure of DNA. The best-selling book appealed to the general public because it dramatically exposed rivalries and Watson's personal feelings about his colleagues. The story revealed that science rarely proceeds in a straightforward manner and has become a classic memoir.

Positions of Influence

In 1968, Watson married Elizabeth Lewis, with whom he had two sons, Rufus Robert and Duncan James. That same year, he became the director of CSHL, where he continued to pursue research in *virology* (the study of viruses), genetics, and cancer. Established in 1889, one of CSHL's missions was the advancement of genetics research. Under Watson's directorship the laboratory's focus expanded to include the study of cancer, and the educational programs flourished. In 1994, Watson became president of CSHL, and today he serves as chancellor. CSHL employs more than 50 research scientists who examine a wide variety of topics in the cell and molecular life sciences and attracts more than 7,000 scientists annually for meetings to communicate the most recent research developments. In 1998, the Watson School of Biological Sciences at CSHL was established as a doctorate degree–granting institution.

From 1988 to 1992, Watson served as associate director and then director of the National Center for Human Genome Research, the division of the National Institutes of Health that oversaw the Human Genome Project. The goal of this endeavor was to completely map and sequence the 3 billion base pairs that constitute the human genome, which was accomplished in 2003. Watson was involved with the scientific research as well as advocating the confrontation of ethical issues it raised. He resigned in 1992 because of policy differences, but he remains a committed spokesperson for the importance of supporting federal funding of scientific research.

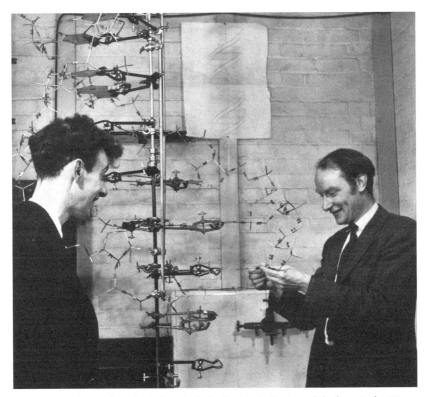

Watson (on the left) and Crick with their double helical model of part of a DNA molecule *(A. Barrington Brown/Photo Researchers, Inc.)*

Watson is recognized as a brilliant scientist and has received numerous prestigious awards in addition to his Nobel Prize, including the Presidential Medal of Freedom (1977) and the National Medal of Science (1997). He belongs to many premier academic organizations including the National Academy of Sciences and the Royal Society of London.

Knowledge of DNA structure was like a key that allowed biologists to unlock doors that exposed several other mysteries of life. During the half century since Watson and Crick solved the double helical puzzle, researchers have defined the physical entity of a gene, learned how DNA codes for the tens of thousands of proteins that constitute organisms, figured out the molecular mechanisms that cause variations leading to the evolution of species, and explained the basis of many inherited diseases. Techniques that have become popular in the last decade, such as cloning, DNA fingerprinting, gene therapy, and genetic engineering, are all possible because Watson paved the way for the molecular revolution in biology. Scientists have sequenced the complete human genome, allowing rapid advances in DNA-based medical procedures, such as estimating the probability of acquiring a specific disease, diagnosing illnesses in order to treat them more effectively, and gene therapy to treat genetic disorders. This profusion of new wisdom brings with it greater responsibility as society makes decisions on the ethical use of the accompanying technology.

CHRONOLOGY

1928	James D. Watson is born on April 6 in Chicago, Illinois
1947	Obtains a bachelor's degree in zoology from the University of Chicago
1950	Receives a doctorate degree in zoology from Indiana University and receives National Research Council Fellowship to conduct research at the University of Copenhagen
1951	Begins postdoctoral research at the Cavendish Laboratory at Cambridge University and starts regular discussions with Francis Crick on the molecular structure of DNA. Attends lec-

	ture on forms of DNA given by Rosalind Franklin at King's College in London
1953	Announces discovery of double helical DNA structure. Publishes landmark paper, "Molecular Structure of Nucleic Acids," in the journal *Nature* with Crick. They publish a second related article discussing implications of the described structure on the function of DNA, "Genetical Implications of the Structure of Deoxyribonucleic Acid," also in *Nature*. Watson becomes a senior research fellow at the California Institute of Technology
1955	Returns to Cavendish Laboratory to collaborate with Crick
1956–76	Researches RNA as a faculty member at Harvard University
1962	Receives Nobel Prize in physiology or medicine shared with Crick and Maurice Wilkins for their discoveries concerning the molecular structure of nucleic acids and its significance for information transfer in living material. Is elected to the National Academy of Sciences
1965	Publishes the first molecular biology textbook, *Molecular Biology of the Gene*
1968	Publishes *The Double Helix*, a narrative about the discovery of the structure of DNA, and becomes director of Cold Spring Harbor Laboratory (CSHL) on Long Island
1988–92	Serves as associate director and then director of the National Center for Human Genome Research
1994	Becomes president of CSHL, then its chancellor
2001	Publishes *Genes, Girls, and Gamow,* a continuation of *The Double Helix* story

FURTHER READING

Adler, Robert E. *Science Firsts: From the Creation of Science to the Science of Creation.* New York: John Wiley, 2002. Stories of 35 landmark scientific discoveries including scientific and historical contexts.

Edelson, Edward. *Francis Crick and James Watson and the Building Blocks of Life.* New York: Oxford University Press, 1998. Biography of the two men whose joint discovery permanently linked their names in the annals of science. Written for young adults.

Horvitz, Leslie Alan. *Eureka! Scientific Breakthroughs that Changed the World.* New York: John Wiley, 2002. Explores the events and thought processes that led 12 great minds to their eureka moments.

McElheny, Victor K. *Watson and DNA: Making a Scientific Revolution.* Cambridge, Mass.: Perseus Publishing, 2003. Biography of Watson, a prime mover of the DNA revolution.

Nobelprize.org. "The Nobel Prize in Physiology or Medicine 1962." Available online. URL: http://www.nobelprize.org/medicine/laureates/1962. Last modified June 16, 2000. Includes links to biographies and Nobel lectures for Watson, Crick, and Wilkins and Nobel lectures.

Watson, James D. *The Double Helix.* New York: Touchstone, 2001. A recent edition of Watson's candid personal and controversial account of the discovery of DNA structure.

GLOSSARY

adenine   one of two nitrogenous purine bases found in nucleic acids

agar   a substance made from red algae that is used as a solidifying agent in microbiological culture media

allele   a form of a gene

anatomy   the study of the structure of an organism

angiosperms   flowering plants

anther   the terminus of a stamen's filament, divided into pollen sacs in which pollen grains form

antibacterial   hostile toward bacteria

antibiotic   a chemical substance made by a microbe that kills or inhibits the growth of other microbes (mainly bacteria)

antibodies   proteins manufactured by the immune system that bind antigens, foreign substances, or microorganisms in order to destroy them or remove them from the body

antiseptic   any chemical substance that kills germs (bacteria, viruses, fungi, etc.)

apothecary   one who prepares and sells medication; a druggist

artery   a vessel that carries blood from the heart throughout the body

artificial selection   process of selective breeding of domesticated plants or animals in which breeders choose the parents to produce the next generation in order to increase the frequency or degree of a particular characteristic

axon   an extension of a neuron that carries nervous signals from the cell body toward the target cells

bacteriology   the study of bacteria

bacteriophage   a virus that infects bacteria

bacterium (plural **bacteria**)   a unicellular, prokaryotic micro-scopic organism

binomial nomenclature   a system of naming organisms with two names, a genus and a species

biophysicist   a scientist who studies the applied laws of physics to explain biological phenomena

blood   the fluid in the arteries, veins, and capillaries that carries nutrients to body tissues and carries waste products away from body tissues

botany   the study of plants

broth   a liquid growth medium

capillaries   tiny blood vessels that connect arteries to veins

carrier   in genetics, an individual who is heterozygous at a given locus, with one normal allele and one potentially harmful reces-sive allele

cell   the smallest structural unit of living matter that can function independently

cell wall   a protective layer external to the plasma or cell mem-brane, found in bacteria, plant cells, fungi, and some protozoans

circulatory system   the organ system in animals responsible for transporting nutrients, carbon dioxide, and waste products throughout the body

community   the populations of plants and animals that live and interact in a defined area such as a pond

complementary   in genetics, two nucleotides, or strands of nucleic acid, that are capable of forming hydrogen bonds between them

corolla   the outer envelope of a flower, composed of fused or sep-arate petals

culture   in microbiology, the artificial growth of microorganisms such as bacteria in a prepared dish in the laboratory

cytosine   one of the nitrogenous pyrimidine bases found in nucleic acid

deoxyribonucleic acid (DNA)   a double-stranded, helical mole-cule that carries the genetic information for an organism and is capable of replicating

differentiation   the structural and functional divergence of cells as they become specialized during development

diploid   having two copies of each chromosome

dissection   the cutting apart of a plant or animal for scientific study

dominant   in genetics, the type of allele that is fully expressed in the phenotype, even in a heterozygote

ecology   the study of the relationships between living creatures and their environments

ecosystem   an ecological community and the physical environment in which it lives

embryology   the study of the formation and development of organisms during the stage following the initiation of *mitosis* in the zygote

entomologist   a scientist who studies insects

epidemic   the rapid spread of a disease, affecting a large segment of a population at one time

ethology   the individual and comparative study of animal behavior

eukaryote   a cell or organism that has a distinct membrane-enclosed nucleus and other membrane-bound organelles

eukaryotic   having a distinct membrane-enclosed nucleus and other membrane-bound organelles

evolution   the change in organisms over time, eventually resulting in the formation of new species

filament   stalklike part of the male reproductive structure of a flower, topped by the anthers

gamete   a *haploid* egg or sperm cell that unites with another gamete during reproduction to form a *diploid* zygote

gene   a discrete unit of hereditary information

genetics   the study of heredity, the passing on of the characteristics of organisms to the offspring

genotype   the genes or alleles that an organism possesses

genus   a taxonomic category just above species

growth factor   a protein that must be present for the normal growth and development of certain types of cells

guanine   one of two nitrogenous purine bases found in nucleic acids

haploid   having only one copy of each chromosome, such as in gametes

heart   the muscular organ that pumps blood throughout the circulatory system by alternatively contracting and expanding

herbarium   collection of pressed and dried plants

heteromorphic   of different form

heterozygous   possessing two different alleles for a given trait

histology   the study of tissue structure at the microscopic level

homologous   in genetics, chromosomes that are essentially identical, carrying the same genes but not necessarily the same alleles

homomorphic   of similar form

homozygous   having two identical alleles for a given trait

humoral   relating to a bodily fluid, such as blood or bile

hybrid   a new variety of plant created by crossing two distinct varieties or species

hydrogen bond   a weak chemical bond formed by the attraction of a slightly positive hydrogen atom with a partially negative atom of another molecule or region of the same molecule

imprinting   a type of learned behavior acquired during a critical period of time, most often referring to learning situations that occur very early in the lives of ground-nesting birds

independent assortment   law of heredity that states that each allele pair segregates independently during gamete formation. This law applies only when the two traits being examined are located on different pairs of *homologous* chromosomes or are sufficiently distant from one another on the same chromosome

infection   the presence in a host of viable microorganisms that cause disease

instinct   a natural tendency to act in a certain way without thinking about it

intravenously   by means of a vein

in vitro   in an artificial environment, such as a test tube, rather than in a living organism

larva (plural **larvae**)   the free-living, wormlike, immature stage of insects and other bugs

lysozyme   an antimicrobial chemical produced by the body that is found in mucus, tears, saliva, and other bodily fluids

magnification the amount by which an optical lens or instrument enlarges an image

medium (plural **media**) a nutritive substance in or on which bacteria, fungi, and other microorganisms are grown for study

meiosis the cellular process of producing haploid gamete cells

meningitis inflammation of the membranes enclosing the brain and spinal cord

microbiology the study of microorganisms, organisms that are too small to be seen by the naked eye

microorganism a living organism too small to be seen by the naked eye

mitosis the process by which a plant or animal cell divides to form two new cells

mold a type of fungus that often grows on bread or fruit. Penicillin was first obtained from the mold *Penicillium*

molecule two or more atoms held together by covalent bonds

motor neuron nerve cell that transmits signals from the brain or spinal cord to muscles or glands

myoglobin a muscle protein that carries oxygen

natural flora microorganisms that colonize a host without causing disease

naturalist someone who studies nature

natural selection the mechanism by which evolution occurs as proposed by Darwin. Those members of a species that survive to breed pass on their genes to their offspring. If the environment changes, only organisms with the appropriate characteristics will survive to pass on their genes. Over time the species may change

nerve growth factor a protein that stimulates the growth of certain types of nerve cells

neuroembryologist one who studies the nervous system in developing unborn animals

neurotransmitter a chemical messenger released from the tip of an axon at a synapse that diffuses across the synapse and stimulates or inhibits the adjacent neuron or effector cell, such as a muscle cell

neurotrophin a member of a family of polypeptides that regulate neuron development and survival

ornithology   the study of birds

ovary   in flowers, the part of the pistil in which the egg-containing ovules develop; in animals, the structure that produces female gametes and reproductive hormones

ovule   the plant structure within the ovary containing the female gametophytes; site of fertilization and seed development

parasitic   obtaining its nutrients from a living host, often causing some harm to the host

pathogenic   causing disease

penicillin   a chemical substance produced by the mold *Penicillium* that has antibacterial properties

petri dish   a circular-shaped plate with a lid that is used to grow bacteria in the laboratory

phagocyte   a type of white blood cell that ingests and digests microorganisms and dead cells

phenotype   the physical and physiological traits of an organism

physiology   the study of the functions of living organisms

pistil   female reproductive structure of a flower, including the stigma, style, and ovary

pollen   an immature male gametophyte that develops in the anthers of flower stamens

preformation   the idea that an entire preformed tiny organism exists inside each egg

prey   any animal hunted by another animal for food

prokaryote   an organism that does not have membrane-enclosed organelles

prokaryotic   having no membrane-enclosed organelles

proliferation   an increase in number, such as by the division of cells or reproduction of organisms

protein   a biomolecule constructed from 20 different amino acids linked by peptide bonds. The chain of amino acids assumes a three-dimensional configuration that determines the protein's function. Proteins perform numerous roles inside the cell

protozoa   a motile eukaryotic organism that does not possess a cell wall or chlorophyll

protozoology   the study of protozoa

pupae   a stage of insect development between the larval stage and adulthood

purine   a class of double-ringed nitrogenous bases found in nucleotides

pyrimidine   a class of single-ringed nitrogenous bases found in nucleotides

receptor   a protein that specifically recognizes and binds another molecule

recessive   an allele or phenotype that does not express itself in the heterozygous condition. It is expressed only in the homozygous form, when a dominant allele is absent

reciprocal cross   a cross with the phenotype of each sex reversed in comparison to the original cross

recombination   in genetics, the process by which homologous chromosomes exchange material during meiosis; crossing over

resolution   the ability of a microscope to distinguish objects separated by small distances

salvarsan   arsphenamine; the first chemotherapeutic drug used to destroy pathogenic microorganisms, discovered in 1910 by Paul Erlich

segregation   law of heredity that states the allele pairs separate during gamete (sex cell) formation and then randomly re-form pairs during the fusion of gametes at fertilization

sensory neuron   nerve cell that receives information from the external or internal environment and transmits signals to the central nervous system

septum   a dividing partition, such as the wall that separates chambers in the heart

sex-linked   genes or traits that are encoded by one of the sex chromosomes, usually the X chromosome

species   a group of organisms that closely resemble one another and are able to interbreed, producing viable, fertile offspring

spermatozoa   the male gamete

spontaneous generation   the production of living organisms from nonliving matter

stamen   male reproductive structure of a flower, including an anther and a filament

staphylococcal   related to staphylococcus

staphylococcus (plural **staphylococci**)   a type of bacteria that is spherical in shape and grows in clusters

stereomicroscope   a microscope that allows the viewer to see an object in three dimensions

stigma   part of the female reproductive structure of a flower to which pollen grains stick, located at the tip of the style

streptococcal   related to streptococcus

streptococcus (plural **streptococci**)   a type of bacteria that is spherical in shape and grows in chains

style   part of the female reproductive structure of a flower, separates the stigma from the ovary

sulfonamides   a class of chemical agents that kill bacteria

synapse   the junction between an axon and a dendrite of an adjacent neuron or an effector cell in a pathway

syphilis   an infectious venereal disease caused by a spirochete bacterium

taxonomy   the scientific study of classifying organisms

thymine   one of two pyrimidine nitrogenous bases found in DNA

tropism   involuntary movement that occurs in living organisms in response to external environmental stimuli, such as light or touch

true-breeding   occurs when self-fertilization gives rise to the same traits in all offspring generation after generation; homozygous

Turner's circling   a behavior exhibited by ants in which they move in circles as they approach a ground nest

vaccine   a weakened or killed bacterium or virus that is injected into a human or animal, stimulating immunity to that particular organism

valve   a moveable part that controls the passage of a fluid, such as a valve that controls blood flow between two chambers in the heart

vein   a vessel that carries blood from the body tissues to the heart

virology   the study of viruses and viral diseases

virulent   dangerous or deadly, such as a harmful strain of a virus

vivisection   the cutting open of a living animal for scientific study or experimentation

X-ray crystallography   a technique used to study the structure of crystallized molecules using X-rays

zoology   the study of animals

FURTHER RESOURCES

Books

American Men and Women in Science. 22nd ed. 8 vols. Detroit: Thomson Gale, 2004. Contains 120,000 short biographical entries in the physical, biological, and related sciences.

The Diagram Group. *The Facts On File Biology Handbook.* New York: Facts On File, 2000. Convenient resource containing a glossary of terms, short biographical profiles of celebrated biologists, a chronology of events and discoveries, and useful charts and tables.

Hine, Robert, ed. *The Facts On File Dictionary of Biology.* 3rd ed. New York: Facts On File, 1999. More than 3,000 entries covering all aspects of biology including organisms, organs, processes, and basic terminology in accessible language.

Kress, John, and Gary W. Barrett, eds. *A New Century of Biology.* Washington, D.C.: Smithsonian Institution Press, 2001. A collection of essays by notable biologists concerning the problems their discipline must address in the 21st century.

Lerner, K. Lee, and Brenda Wilmoth Lerner, eds. *Gale Encyclopedia of Science.* 3rd ed. 6 vols. Detroit: Thomson Gale, 2003. Provides an overview of current scientific knowledge, consisting of alphabetical entries of scientific concepts and terms. Written for young adults.

Mendelsohn, Everett, ed. *Life Sciences before the Twentieth Century: Biographical Portraits.* New York: Scribner, 2001. Survey of 90 men and women who made important discoveries in a variety of life science fields before the 20th century. Written for young adults.

————, ed. *Life Sciences in the Twentieth Century: Biographical Portraits.* New York: Scribner, 2000. Survey of 90 men and women who made important discoveries in a variety of life science fields during the 20th century. Written for young adults.

Narins, Brigham, ed. *Notable Scientists: From 1900 to the Present.* 2nd ed. 5 vols. Farmington Hills, Mich.: Thomson Gale, 2000. Contains 1,600 biographical profiles of scientists in the natural, physical, and applied sciences.

Rittner, Don, and Timothy L. McCabe. *Encyclopedia of Biology.* New York: Facts On File, 2004. Comprehensive reference of 800 A-to-Z entries encompassing definitions, issues, discoveries, biographies, and experiments.

Robinson, Richard, ed. *Biology.* 4 vols. New York: Macmillan Reference USA, 2001. Explains biological concepts, reviews history of biology, and explores related fields. Written for young adults.

Yount, Lisa. *A to Z of Biologists.* New York: Facts On File, 2003. Profiles more than 150 biologists, discussing their research and contributions. Includes bibliography, glossary, cross-references, and chronology.

Internet Resources

ASU Ask a Biologist. Arizona State University. Available online. URL: http://askabiologist.asu.edu. Modified on January 3, 2005. Intended as a resource for K–12 students and teachers.

Bio: Directorate for Biological Sciences. The National Science Foundation. Available online. URL: http://www.nsf.gov/bio. Last modified on September 3, 2004. Explore the Web site to learn about current biology news, recent press releases, NSF divisions and programs, and funding information.

Biointeractive. Howard Hughes Medical Institute, 2004. Available online. URL: http://www.hhmi.org/biointeractive. Accessed on January 14, 2005. Contains animations, virtual labs, and lectures on a variety of current topics including cancer, DNA, infectious diseases, and more.

Biology Online. Available online. URL: http://www.biology-online. org. Accessed on January 14, 2005. Organized into three sections: "Dictionary of Biology," "Biology Tutorials," and "Biology on the Web."

The Biology Project. Available online. URL: http://www.biology. arizona.edu. Revised July 2004. An interactive online resource for learning biology, developed at the University of Arizona, that contains numerous activities, tutorials, and additional Internet resources.

Farabee, M. J. *Online Biology Book*. 2002. Available online. URL: http://www.emc.maricopa.edu/faculty/farabee/BIOBK/Bio BookTOC.html. Accessed January 14, 2005. Developed by an introductory biology college teacher, this e-book is organized into chapters, including diagrams and links to glossary terms.

Gilbert, Joanna. "BiologyMad." Available online. URL: http:// www.biologymad.com. Accessed on January 14, 2005. Contains topic notes, concept maps, and animations on subjects including cells, genetics, human biology, biochemistry, ecosystems and the environment, and plant biology.

Kimball, John W. *Kimball's Biology Pages*. 2005. Available online. URL: http://biology-pages.info. A regularly updated, online biology text based on Wm. C. Brown's 1994 edition, written by a Harvard University faculty member.

National Institutes of Health Office of Science Education homepage. Available online. URL: http://science.education.nih.gov. Accessed on January 14, 2005. Follow links under "Educational Resources" for students or for the public.

NewScientist.com. Available online. URL: http://www.newscientist. com. Accessed on January 14, 2005. Comprehensive coverage of current science and technology news.

Online Mendelian Inheritance in Man, OMIM. McKusick-Nathans Institute for Genetic Medicine, Johns Hopkins University (Baltimore, Md.) and National Center for Biotechnology Information, National Library of Medicine (Bethesda, Md.), 2000. Available online. URL: http://www.ncbi.nlm.nih.gov/ omim. Accessed on January 14, 2005. Contains links to enormous amounts of technical information regarding genetic disorders, locations of specific genes, statistics, and genome databases.

Science and Nature: Prehistoric Life: Beasts: Evolution. British Broadcasting Corporation. Available online. URL: http://www.bbc.co.uk/beasts/evolution. Accessed on January 14, 2005. Access to an online game where the player becomes a small primate 50 million years ago and must adapt to changes in the environment in order to survive and to a fish-zapping experiment that illustrates evolution.

Sullivan, James A. Cells Alive! Quill Graphics, 2003. Available online. URL: http://www.cellsalive.com. Accessed on January 14, 2005. Contains links to illustrations, micrographs, animations of cells and their processes, biological structures, and quizzes.

Periodicals

BioScience

Published by the American Institute of Biological Sciences
1444 I Street NW, Suite 200
Washington, DC 20005
Telephone: (202) 628-1500
Monthly journal containing overviews of current research in biology. Written for researchers, educators, and students.

Discover

Published by Buena Vista Magazines
114 Fifth Avenue
New York, NY 10011
Telephone: (212) 633-4400
www.discover.com
A popular monthly magazine containing easy-to-understand articles on a variety of scientific topics.

Frontiers in Bioscience

Published by Frontiers in Bioscience
P.O. Box 160
Albertson, NY 11507-0160
Telephone: (516) 484-2831
www.bioscience.org

An online journal and virtual library with articles covering all disciplines in biology.

Journal of Biology

Published by BioMed Central Ltd.
Middlesex House
34-42 Cleveland Street
London W1T 4LB UK
Telephone: +44 (0)20 7323 0323
http://jbiol.com
Publishes original research articles both in print and on the Web (freely available to all).

Nature

The Macmillan Building
4 Crinan Street
London N1 9XW UK
Telephone: +44 (0)20 7833 4000
www.nature.com/nature
A prestigious primary source of scientific literature.

Science

Published by the American Association for the Advancement of Science
1200 New York Avenue NW
Washington, DC 20005
Tel: (202) 326-6417
www.sciencemag.org
One of the most highly regarded primary sources for scientific literature.

Scientific American

415 Madison Avenue
New York, NY 10017
Telephone: (212) 754-0550
www.sciam.com

A popular monthly magazine that publishes articles on a broad range of subjects and current issues in science and technology.

Societies and Organizations

American Association for the Advancement of Science (www.aaas.org), 1200 New York Avenue NW, Washington, DC 20005. Telephone: 202-326-6400

American Institute of Biological Sciences (www.aibs.org), 1444 I Street NW, Suite 200, Washington, DC 20005. Telephone: (202) 628-1500

Federation of American Societies for Experimental Biology (www.faseb.org), 9650 Rockville Pike, Bethesda, MD 20814. Telephone: (301) 634-7000

The Human Biology Association (www.humbio.org), c/o Ted Steegmann, President (2003–07), Department of Anthropology, University at Buffalo, 380 MFAC, Buffalo, NY 14261. Telephone: (716) 645-2240

The Linnean Society of London (www.linnean.org), Burlington House, Picadilly, London, W1J 0BF, UK. Telephone: +44 020 7434 4479

Index